W9-APM-862

Classroom Practices
in Teaching English
1979–1980

NCTE Committee on Classroom Practices in Teaching English

Gene Stanford, Child Life and Education Department, The
    Children's Hospital of Buffalo, Chair
Jeffrey N. Golub, Kent Junior High School, Washington
Jane Hornburger, City University of New York
Raymond J. Rodrigues, University of Utah
Frances Russell, Winchester Schools, Massachusetts, *ex officio*
Charles Suhor, NCTE Staff Liaison
Ouida H. Clapp, Buffalo Board of Education, New York, consultant

Classroom Practices
in Teaching English
1979–1980

How to Handle
the Paper Load

Gene Stanford, Chair,
and the Committee on Classroom Practices

National Council of Teachers of English
1111 Kenyon Road, Urbana, Illinois 61801

NCTE Editorial Board: Paul T. Bryant, Thomas J. Creswell, C. Kermeen Fristrom, Rudine Sims, Ann Terry, Robert F. Hogan, *ex officio*, Paul O'Dea, *ex officio*

Book Design: Tom Kovacs, interior; V. Martin, cover

NCTE Stock Number 06897

© 1979 by the National Council of Teachers of English. All rights reserved. Printed in the United States of America.

It is the policy of NCTE in its journals and other publications to provide a forum for the open discussion of ideas concerning the content and the teaching of English and the language arts. Publicity accorded to any particular point of view does not imply endorsement by the Executive Committee, the Board of Directors, or the membership at large, except in announcements of policy where such endorsement is clearly specified.

Library of Congress Cataloging in Publication Data

Main entry under title:

How to handle the paper load.

    (Classroom practices in teaching English, 1979–1980)
    Bibliography: p.
    1. English language—Study and teaching (Secondary)
2. English language—Rhetoric.   3. Report writing—
Evaluation.   4. Copy-reading.   I. Stanford, Gene.
II. National Council of Teachers of English.
Committee on Classroom Practices.   III. Series.
LB1631.H76   808′.042′0712   79-22498
ISBN 0-8141-0689-7

Contents

Preface

The need for specific ways to teach writing skills effectively at a time when class sizes are unacceptably large in many schools was the dominant theme of the open meeting of the Committee on Classroom Practices in Teaching English held in Kansas City on November 23, 1978. Although only four members of the Council joined the three members of the Committee for the open meeting, the discussion of issues facing English teachers was lively and wide-ranging. By consensus the group chose "How to Handle the Paper Load" as the theme for the 1979–80 publication.

During the closed meeting, committee members established explicit criteria for evaluating manuscripts (appropriateness to theme, pedagogical soundness, quality of presentation, freshness, and practicality) and a new rating scale (definitely use, maybe use, I don't care, don't use, never ever use). Promptly after the meeting, invitations for manuscripts on handling the paper load were issued in *Language Arts*, *The English Journal*, *Council-Grams*, *College English*, and *English Education*, and in the journals of numerous NCTE-affiliated organizations.

By the April 15 deadline, 127 manuscripts were submitted by educators in thirty-nine states and Canada. The manuscripts, with authors' names removed, were evaluated by committee members Jane Hornburger, Jeffrey N. Golub, Raymond J. Rodrigues, and the chair—a committee representing different geographical areas and a variety of viewpoints at several educational levels.

Twenty-seven manuscripts were ultimately selected for publication and approved by the Council's Editorial Board. Although the approaches they describe vary as widely as the geographical regions and educational settings in which their authors work, all reveal that members of the profession are devising creative ways of teaching writing well even though confronted with unreasonably large classes.

Introduction

Imagine that your mother is recovering from surgery and is expected to be in the hospital at least a week. The hospital is an hour away from your home, and you have 150 compositions to grade this week. What do you do? Choose one:

a. Tell your mother that you are sorry, but you can visit her only once during her stay.

b. Tell your students that you are sorry, but that their compositions will not be returned until late next week.

c. "Fake" grading the papers by randomly writing letter grades at the top and jotting comments such as "good idea," "this paragraph needs development," and "try for a better conclusion."

Or imagine that on a Tuesday night you come home with a splitting headache and forty-five compositions to grade. You are also teaching the third act of *Macbeth* tomorrow, and you have not read it since you left college. What do you do? Choose one:

a. Forget the papers and read *Macbeth*.

b. Grade the compositions and read the Monarch Notes on *Macbeth*.

c. Go to bed and hope for a blizzard that will close school for a day or two.

Or imagine that your fiance has invited you to go skiing over the weekend at a posh resort 150 miles from home. But quarter grades are due on Monday, and you have saved up three sets of twenty-five papers each to grade. What do you do? Choose one:

a. Tell your fiance that you now understand why teachers in the old days were expected to take a vow of celibacy as well as poverty, and so you have decided to give up the relationship and all social life and devote yourself exclusively to teaching.

b. Tell your fiance that since it appears that you have to choose between romance and teaching, you have decided to quit your job.

c. Go skiing and grade papers while waiting in the lift line.

If you are an English teacher, you are probably no stranger to the kind of dilemmas described above. Simple mathematics shows that the job of teaching English, at least considering present-day realities, may not be humanly possible. Most members of the profession would agree that it takes at least ten minutes to respond well to a student's composition. If you have four classes totaling 100 students, the number endorsed by NCTE as the maximum load, and you assign a composition to all classes, you will need approximately seventeen hours to respond to all of them. By having students write a composition only every second week, you could complete your paper grading by spending one hour a day on weekdays and two hours on weekends. Not a completely unreasonable expectation.

But these are calculations based on the ideal, and ideal circumstances are hard to find these days. At the same time that the public has been pushing for more emphasis on the teaching of writing, it has also been opposing tax hikes, with the result that most teachers now have far more than the recommended number of students. Five classes a day with thirty students is a more common figure. With this class load you must spend a total of twenty-five hours responding to a composition by every student or almost two hours per day of grading, even if students write only once every two weeks.

And of course, other duties are not lessened. You must still prepare for classes. If you include rereading literary works, designing an overall unit plan, and selecting the day's methods and materials, preparing lessons probably requires an average of an hour per lesson. If you have five classes a day with three preparations, you could easily spend three hours a day in lesson planning. Added to the time spent responding to compositions, that totals five hours of work to do after the typical seven-hour school day is over. And that figure does not include time for other school-related responsibilities, such as sponsoring extra-curricular activities, that the conscientious teacher wants to assume.

Furthermore, good teachers know the extreme importance of maintaining enough family, social, and personal time to assure good mental and physical health, for no amount of careful grading and thorough planning can compensate for physical and mental exhaustion. No wonder that members of the profession feel engulfed in a no-win situation, caught between taxpayers' demands for improved performance and the impossibility of the task. No wonder that frustration has increased as teachers are forced to choose which aspects of their jobs they will do well and which they will do poorly, because it does not seem humanly possible to do it all.

Pressing for reduced student loads is ultimately the only way out of the dilemma, and certainly NCTE must continue its efforts to this end untiringly. But, as Thomas Newkirk points out in his article in this volume, this is a battle the profession has waged since at least 1912, and with few apparent results. Since Edwin Hopkins asked "Can Good Composition Teaching Be Done Under Present Conditions?" in the very first issue of *The English Journal*, the profession has argued continuously and fervently for reasonable class loads, but circumstances have remained virtually unchanged to this day. Clearly, at least for the immediate future, we must look elsewhere for a solution.

The contributors to this volume, in seeking that solution in their own classrooms, have discovered that we must reexamine the methodologies we have used for teaching writing. They point out that although the public's concern about writing skills has led us to recommit ourselves to teaching composition conscientiously, we have continued to use methodologies that produce an enormous paper load and which may not have been the most effective anyway. We have continued to rely on what Marilou Sorensen and Margo Sorgman have dubbed the "Assign-Assess Syndrome," hoping that if we just assign more papers to be written and assess the quality of those papers, writing skills will naturally improve. If students are not developing skills fast enough by writing every other week, we think perhaps we should require a composition *weekly*. And thereby we double the paper load with no assurance that improved writing skills will result.

The "assign-assess" approach is based on the assumption that writing skills are best developed by a teacher's assigning a paper and, after the paper is written, assessing the student's performance. Put more specifically, we are clinging to a myth—that to learn to write well, students must always write whole compositions in which every error is marked by the teacher and that the teacher does not respond to the writing until a finished product is submitted. Authors of the articles in this volume have discovered that by questioning various components of this myth they can foster growth in composition even more successfully than through the "assign-assess" approach and at the same time save themselves from an avalanche of papers to grade.

They have discovered, for example, that not everything that a student writes must be graded, or even read, in order to have an effect on the student's skill development. Free-writing, journals, and a number of other nongraded activities can give students the practice and the freedom to experiment that weekly compositions cannot always provide.

The contributors also have discovered that teachers can best serve their students by being actively involved as consultants during the writing process rather than waiting until a finished product is submitted for grading. These authors have devised a number of ways to become directly involved in the writing process—lab tactics, role playing, writing along with their students—instead of merely making an assignment and waiting for a set of papers to grade.

Still others have learned that teaching students how to identify and correct weaknesses in their own work before submitting it reduces the amount of time teachers must spend in annotating papers. By teaching students to serve as their own editors, these teachers relieve themselves of the need to spend endless hours editing student work.

Some contributors have reconsidered the need for assigning full-length compositions every time they want to give students practice. They have concluded that it is sometimes more effective and less time-consuming for students to practice with shorter forms or with particular aspects of writing. These teachers have discovered that by identifying the specific skills they wish to teach and by sequencing these carefully, they can often accomplish as much by having students make a list or write a single paragraph as by writing a whole essay. For example, a teacher who wants students to learn how to develop a general idea with specific details can in the beginning stages assign self-checking exercises in which students supply a list of specifics for each general idea. The danger exists, of course, that such an approach will limit writing to fill-in-the-blanks exercises and never give students an opportunity to master longer compositions. When used wisely, however, it can teach specific skills without demanding that the teacher respond to only full-length compositions.

Another component of the "assign-assess" myth that the contributors address is that every error must be marked in order for students to improve their writing. Many English teachers have learned from both psychological research and their own common sense that overuse of the red pen produces little more than disgust in students and writer's cramp in teachers. Focusing on a few errors that can be corrected by students at their present level of skill is usually far more effective than flooding students with more feedback than they can possibly assimilate.

Finally, some contributors have discovered that the teacher does not have to be the only source of feedback for students. Other students can respond to the work of their peers. In fact, peer reactions are often more effective, both because most young people value the opinions of their peers more than those of their teachers and because a student can often understand the writing problems faced by a fellow student better than the teacher, who cannot recall the time when he or she did not know what a sentence or a paragraph was. The uses of peer evaluation and the extent to which students are given responsibility for determining grades can vary widely, of course, depending on the type of students and the purposes of the activity.

But the articles contributed to this volume bear testimony to more than teachers' ingenuity in coping successfully with the paper load. They illustrate the important principle that when forced to grapple with a particular problem, human beings often discover solutions that pay dividends far beyond just eliminating the original problem. For example, in attempting to solve the problem of railroad lanterns that cracked under extreme weather conditions, scientists at Corning Glass produced Pyrex, which is now in use in millions of kitchens and laboratories throughout the world. In the case of teaching writing, the problem of the paper load has encouraged teachers to be their most creative and effective, and the strategies they have put into practice in their classrooms, rather than being corner-cutting methods, are actually bringing better results than the old "assign-assess" procedures. Thus, both the survival of the teacher and the writing skills of students are equally benefitted by the approaches described by these contributors. Faced with class sizes that are larger than they should be and bound by a renewed commitment to teaching composition well, teachers have taken a second look at the traditional ways of teaching writing, and as a result they have developed new strategies that provide the soundest possible instruction under circumstances that are at best difficult.

Gene Stanford
Chair

1 Ungraded Writing

Writing Roulette: Taking a Chance on Not Grading

R. Baird Shuman
University of Illinois at Urbana-Champaign

Not all student writing needs to be graded. This statement may sound like heresy to the traditional teacher, but consider it in relation to the problem of achieving fluency in writing. Many students have difficulty just getting words down on paper in sufficient volume to write even a five paragraph theme in fifty minutes. Many such students are lacking in fluency because they have nothing they really wish to write about. Some are not fluent because they are too afraid of making errors in spelling or in the mechanics of expression and for this reason lose their forward thrust. Others just feel no urgency about putting ideas down on paper. Writing roulette is one activity that stimulates such students and helps them to overcome these problems. As you will see, it is impossible to grade the papers which grow from this activity, although most teachers will want to glance over them.

In order to play writing roulette you need a classful of kids, a sheet of paper and a pencil for each of them and for yourself, and a kitchen timer. Then announce: "Today all of us will write. When I say, 'Go!' start writing about anything that comes to mind. The object is to fill as much of the paper as you can. Do not worry about spelling or punctuation. Just write, write, write until the timer sounds. Then stop even if you are in the middle of a word. If you cannot think of anything to write about, select a word that appeals to you—*dinosaur* or *petunia* or *Penelope*—and write it over and over. The object, remember, is to fill as much of the paper as you can in the time allotted. GO!"

Set the timer for two minutes and write along with the students. When the timer sounds, say: "Stop writing and pass your papers ahead." When you have the papers, redistribute them so that everyone has someone else's paper. Then announce, "Read what is written on the paper you have, and add to it. Write until the timer sounds. GO!'' Set the timer for about two and one-half minutes to allow time for reading the first contribution. Repeat this exercise three or four times, increasing the interval by about thirty seconds each time so that students are able to read the papers before them. Finally, ask several students to read aloud the papers to which they were the last contributors.

Students like this activity so well that they beg to do it again and again, and through it they gain excellent practice in writing rapidly. A proofreading session may be held the following day, going through the papers to correct punctuation, spelling, agreement, and the like. Practice in editing could also grow out of the activity. Each student may be asked to unify his or her paper to make it read as though all its parts had been written by the same person. Writing roulette and its follow-up exercises achieve legitimate and necessary pedagogical ends but, at the same time, need not require intensive reading and grading by the teacher.

The Journal: A Practical Option for Teaching Writing

Thomas R. Moore
Wachusett Regional High School

Joseph Reynolds
Wachusett Regional High School

Mark Harris, novelist and essayist, gives this advice to prospective writers: "Grow ears." All great writers are listeners and observers, collectors of anecdotes, words, phrases, and metaphors that are ever present in their experience. And where better to collect these tidbits than in a journal? Thoreau, whose *Walden* grew out of his journal, has this to say about journal writing:

> . . . a journal is a repository for all those fragmentary ideas and odd scraps of information that might otherwise be lost and which someday might lead to more "harmonious" compositions.

No greater authority than Thoreau need be mentioned in support of journal writing.

An obvious advantage of the journal in high school composition classes is that the teacher need not read everything that students write, yet they continue to write and, we hope, their writing improves with practice. Keeping a journal encourages students to think about their individual writing problems and to work on solutions on a daily basis. Journal writing also has all the advantages of free-writing, a technique of writing so eloquently espoused by Peter Elbow. He suggests that one write freely and spontaneously until one hits upon a core idea. This idea then becomes the source for something that can be more finely polished and presented to an audience—the class and the teacher—or even published. Finally, journal writing takes place in a relaxed but serious atmosphere where ideas can flow readily onto the page, and students need not worry about grammar or diction. The editorial work is done in the rewriting process.

Journal Project

1. In what ways are you similar to a three year old?
2. Do you want to go to college and/or get married?
3. Why are myths important?
4. Do you want to learn the truth?
5. Why do artists often lead difficult lives?
6. What do you dream about?
7. How would you deal with divorce?
8. How do you deal with frustration?
9. What is one small change that you promise, now, to make in your life?
10. What are your feelings about taking drugs?
11. What is infatuation?
12. How would you deal with the death of someone close to you?
13. Which impressionist painter do you react to the most?
14. In what ways are you creative?
15. What is quality?
16. What do you fear most?
17. How important is religion in your life?
18. How could your parents best teach you to be a responsible person?
19. What is courage?
20. What poem has changed your life?

Pact

I promise to

1. use the specified loose leaf binder,
2. set aside time each week to write,
3. write on at least ten of the suggested topics,
4. bring the journal to class each Friday,
5. write a summary for the last entry, noting particularly any changes in attitude,
6. be truthful.

It is understood that the journal will be your private thoughts and need only be shown to Mr., Mrs., Ms. _____ .

Signed _____   Date _____

Attach This to Your Journal

One journal writing option, and the one we most frequently use, is to ask students to write for ten minutes on a topic suggested by the teacher: Describe your bedroom; Describe the object you own that you treasure most; How can your parents teach you to be responsible? After giving five such assignments on five consecutive days, ask each student to select his or her best piece of writing, to rewrite it, and to pass it in for a grade.

A second option requires students to write once a week at home in a quiet place. Here, the student is given a list of writing topics and signs a contract. (A copy of the contract and the list of topics appears on p. 6.) The topics are broad in scope and encourage students to explore themselves, their values, and their environments. Writing in their journals about a provocative question helps students to see their positions more clearly and even to discover new ideas. Class discussions on controversial issues are healthier and more dynamic if students have first written about these issues in their journals. It is useful if the teacher collects the journals at intervals, reads some entries, and makes brief comments. Students crave teacher comments however brief.

A common argument teachers offer against journal writing is that they will learn things they don't want to know: "Lisa's afraid she's pregnant," "Jim's parents have discussed divorce," "Marianne has considered suicide." Such entries, as a matter of fact, are rare but may be cries for help which require a response— a short talk and suggestions where to find help if needed. The topic list, however, helps to steer students away from overly personal areas.

Over the course of the term, we develop a list of good writing habits that are gleaned from class discussions on writing and journal keeping. Our students can always look forward to a mid-term or final exam question that requires a supporting essay from their journals.

Journal writing does keep students writing while at the same time reducing the burden of grades for teachers, but perhaps an even stronger justification for including it in the writing curriculum is the opportunity it offers students and teachers to get to know each other. We have discovered that students who are too shy to share their experiences in class often write about them in interesting, even dynamic entries. A teacher should love writing and love to talk about what makes good writing. Student journals allow teachers to do this on a consistent basis, and their enthusiasm often becomes contagious.

Theodore Roethke, major American poet and inveterate journal writer, left behind some two hundred notebooks and journals full of lines, images, and ideas, some of which he had already turned into poems. He wrote in these notebooks an important gloss on his poetry—and without these journals, it would have been lost—"The Greenhouse: my symbol for the whole of life, a womb, a heaven-on-earth." Journal keeping, as the work of Roethke and Thoreau attests, is a valid means of discovering oneself, of refining new ideas, and of sustaining the habit of writing. Surely, then, the journal is a valid means of teaching writing.

Journals:
Write More—Grade Less

Jane Zeni Flinn
University of Missouri at St. Louis
and Instructor, "Writing for Teachers" workshop
for the Gateway Writing Project

We learn to write by writing—and by receiving feedback. But responding to papers takes time, and too often teachers have resorted to the principle, "Write less—grade less," with tragic results. Mina Shaughnessy points out that "compared with the 1000 words a week that a British student is likely to have written in the equivalent of an American high school or even the 350 words a week that an American student in a middle-class high school is likely to have written, the basic writing student is more likely to have written 350 words a semester" (*Errors and Expectations*, p. 14). If we believe with James Britton that a writing teacher's basic job is to "keep the flow going" and if we are not to be swamped by a torrent of prose, we will have to adopt the slogan, "Write more—grade less." Our students will do pages of writing that will not be dissected with the infamous red pen, but writing nonetheless that can help them develop fluency and confidence. But how, exactly, do we start this flow of writing?

I thought that journals were the obvious answer, yet they had never worked in my classes. Students regarded my journal assignments as busy work and filled their pages with the trivia of breakfasts and bus rides or with the superficial details of their romances. What they wrote in their journals had no relation at all to their "real" papers.

Then I examined my own method of writing. Like my students, I am terrified of a blank page—but unlike them, I rarely sit down to one. I always carry a notebook for jotting down ideas as they occur to me, and when I actually sit down to write, I have page upon comforting page of material to work with. (I asked about this blank page syndrome at a writing workshop recently and learned that most members of the group practiced similar forms of prewriting.) Couldn't my students learn to use journals in this way?

Eventually I introduced a structured kind of journal writing as an integral part of the composing process.* My students fill page after page in response to the familiar directive: "Write about your observations and experiences each day." But now I ask about their experiences, not only with people and places, but also with ideas—with opposing theories based on the same empirical data or with a false analogy lurking at the root of an argument. In addition, their entries now have a focus, since each journal chapter feeds into one "official" course paper. This approach means more writing and less grading, since I write detailed comments only on the final papers.

Journal Assignments

The following journal assignments generate the material for papers often assigned in freshman composition courses. Most can be adapted for basic or advanced college writers, for high school students, or for English teachers.

I. Description

Journal (in class): Develop a feel for concrete detail through exercises in close observation of interesting objects. (See George Hillocks, *Observing and Writing.*)

Journal (outside class): (1) Be a Five Senses Tape Recorder. Write quickly, recording exactly what you see, hear, smell, taste, and feel: slush seeping through winter galoshes; coffee break chatter; sweet apple crisp and dull diet fare; your pen's shadow crawling across a page. (2) Write about your day, but move beyond simple chronology by trying to capture sense impressions and moods. Draw your reader into your experience.

Paper: Describe a person or an object that is special to you.

II. Autobiography

Journal (in class): (1) Relax, close your eyes, and imagine yourself as a young child. Focus on one scene and write quickly, trying to recapture how you felt at the time. (2) Draw a "life line,"

---

*Sandra Albright, Joyce Jeffries, and Kenneth Van Buren of the Gateway Writing Project started me thinking about structured journals.

labeling events that had a lasting impact on you. (See Richard Beach, *Writing about Ourselves and Others.*)

Journal (outside class): Write about one such recollection from childhood each day for a week—or for two weeks.

Paper: Choose the best journal entry and write an autobiographical sketch that captures a scene from your childhood.

III. Literary Analysis

(My students choose a book from a list of well-written autobiographies, but this assignment could be based on other literary types.)

Journal (in class): Choose a scene that made a strong impression on you and record all the vivid, concrete words, phrases, and images. Now look for a pattern among these words. Can you classify your entries according to more general concepts? (Try the method of naming, opposing, and defining in Ann Berthoff's *Forming, Thinking, Writing: The Composing Imagination.*)

Journal (outside): Analyze several scenes from the autobiography you have read, trying to discover *why* the writer has presented these word-pictures.

Paper: (1) Develop your best journal entry into an analytical essay; show how your writer has used vivid, sensory language to develop a theme. (2) Any other open-ended question may be explored in journal entries and then developed into a paper.

IV. Writing in Style

Journal (in class): (1) Translate a visual image into *one* sentence of prose. (Paintings by Breughel and Chagall and photographs from *Family of Man* work well.) (2) Develop syntactic fluency by imitating a variety of sentences written by professionals. (See James Gray, "Teaching the New Rhetoric," and Francis Christensen, *Notes Toward a New Rhetoric.*)

Journal (outside): (1) Continue to record your observations of people and places with your Five Senses Tape Recorder, but this week, distill your impressions into one or two flowing, cumulative sentences. (2) Now try some longer scenes, but continue to work on effectiveness of individual sentences.

Paper: Develop your best entry into a feature article describing an action-filled scene—a political rally, a disco, a laundromat, a funeral.

V. Research Paper

(To avoid the dreary library report, I encourage students to choose topics they already know and care about, topics they can investigate first hand as well as through published sources.)

Research Journal: (1) For each published source, record bibliographic data, short summary, and quotations. As you write, *think* about the ideas and how they relate to other material you have encountered. Respond by inserting your own questions and comments. (2) Record interviews and direct observation, again with your own comments. (3) Grapple with a thesis, organize an outline, and write at least two drafts.

Paper: Turn in the related journal entries with your completed research paper. (A five-page paper is often accompanied by forty pages of journal. It takes me about five minutes to leaf through the journal entries, and because the writer had to think, not just record, the paper itself tends to be worth reading.)

VI. *Argument Analysis*

(Students are asked to read a group of argument essays; they are also urged to re-examine articles they read for their research papers. A sample argument is analyzed in class.)

Journal: Each day comment on one essay. Look for the writer's voice, intended audience, and purpose. What assumptions does the writer make? What evidence does the writer offer? What fallacies detract from the argument? Would the essay convince its audience? Does it convince you? (These entries are written schematically.)

Paper: Use your best journal entry as the basis for a paper that analyzes how an argument worked or failed to work.

VII. *Persuasive Essay*

(Students are asked to choose an issue with which they are already involved, one they can present convincingly to members of their writing class.)

Journals: (1) Write quickly about the issue to generate your own ideas and feelings. (2) Read up on the issue, recording your notes and comments as for a research paper. (3) Choose a published source you strongly disagree with, and talk back in detail. (4) Explain your position on the issue to at least three different audiences. (5) After completing the first draft of your paper, look back and consider your own persuasive style. Is your voice formal, intimate, objective, sarcastic, pleading? Smooth out any inconsistencies in your voice. (6) Can you strengthen your essay with vivid sensory detail, sharply-drawn scenes, natural dialogue, and varied, mature sentence structure?

Paper: Show off by writing a *persuasive* essay. Convince us with your logic and delight us with your rhetoric.

Responding to Journals

Journal assignments can be tailored to suit virtually any paper. At the same time, I believe the journals are important in their own right, not merely as practice for the finished essays. I encourage my students, even while working on research and argument papers, to save a page or two of their journals each week to record a striking scene or a moving experience. Because the journals are important in their own right, they are assessed at the end of the course for 20 percent of the final grade. This grade is not, of course, awarded for polished form, but for consistent practice and a willingness to experiment.

My students have been willing to keep journals going with a modest amount of feedback. At the beginning of the course I collect the journals every week or ten days; later, when the writing has its own momentum, I allow several weeks between readings. I respond to the journals in a number of ways. Sometimes I ditto choice excerpts, especially during the first weeks when we are trying to establish the qualities of clear, vivid, effective writing. (See Ken Macrorie, *Telling Writing.*) Other times, I write a few comments in the margins or a brief note at the end of their journals. These responses are always positive and very specific—praise for a sparkling sentence, a suggestion for next week's journal. Often I simply glance at the journals and check them off as students work in groups on the entries they will develop into finished papers. In this case, a certain number of journal entries may be required as an admission ticket to the editing groups. (See Thom Hawkins, *Group Inquiry Techniques for Teaching Writing.*)

Whatever the method, I can respond to a journal in a fraction of the time it takes me to respond to a paper. A structured journal is a non-threatening form of writing practice, but it is not busy work. Through journals, my students now spend a major portion of their composition time on prewriting and planning; their drafts show more thought, and the finished products really look finished. Students write more, but I grade less.

References

Beach, Richard. *Writing about Ourselves and Others.* Urbana, Ill.: NCTE/ERIC, 1977.

Berthoff, Ann E. *Forming, Thinking, Writing: The Composing Imagination.* Rochelle Park, N.J.: Hayden Book Co., 1977.

Britton, James. *Language and Learning.* New York: Penguin, 1970.

Christensen, Francis. *Notes Toward a New Rhetoric.* New York: Harper and Row, 1967.

Gray, James. "Teaching the New Rhetoric." Unpublished Bay Area Writing Project guide.

Hawkins, Thom. *Group Inquiry Techniques for Teaching Writing.* Urbana, Ill.: NCTE/ERIC, 1976.

Hillocks, George. *Observing and Writing.* Urbana, Ill.: NCTE/ERIC, 1975.

Macrorie, Ken. *Telling Writing.* Rochelle Park, N.J.: Hayden Book Co., 1973.

Shaughnessy, Mina. *Errors and Expectations: A Guide for the Teacher of Basic Writing.* New York: Oxford University Press, 1977.

Journal Writing Across the Curriculum

Toby E. Fulwiler
Michigan Technological University

> When I write a paper I make it personal. I put myself into it and I
> write well. It bothers me when people tell me to make it more
> impersonal—to take *me* out of it. I'm afraid I can't write unless I
> am in the paper somehow.
>
> Jody S.

Writing is a learning tool with a place in every academic classroom.
It is not the sole province of the English teacher any more than
numbers are strictly the math teacher's responsibility, or speaking,
the speech teacher's. Over a decade ago, Dan Fader called for
"English in Every Classroom," arguing that only when teachers in
all disciplines emphasize the importance of good writing will students, in turn, recognize its value.[1] A common objection to Fader's
position raised by classroom teachers is the amount of time it
takes to assign and evaluate student writing, especially in large
classes. However, recent composition theory supports, more
strongly than ever, the importance of the writing students do
strictly for themselves, writing the teacher need never see nor formally evaluate. I'm speaking, of course, about student journals, a
time-honored form of writing which, when well used, is capable of
revolutionizing classroom learning. This paper argues that assigning
journals increases writing fluency, facilitates learning, and pro-
motes cognitive growth, regardless of class size or disciplinary spe-
cialization.

Expressive Writing

Research by James Britton and his colleagues at the University
of London suggests that the writing taught in schools today is
narrowly conceived. In looking at 2,000 pieces of writing from
sixty-five secondary schools Britton's researchers categorized the

writing as (1) transactional, (2) poetic, or (3) expressive.[2] Transactional writing gets things done; it informs, instructs, persuades, and carries on business. Most writing required in schools is transactional: term papers, lab reports, essay tests, and book reviews. Poetic writing is art; *how* something is said becomes as important as *what* is said. Teachers often call this kind of writing "creative" and limit it to poetry, fiction, and drama. Expressive writing reveals the thinking process; it is often unstructured and close to informal speech; diaries, journals, personal letters, and first drafts are examples. Teachers seldom encourage expressive writing, especially in the higher grades, since this form accounted for less than four percent of senior high school writing in Britton's study. Britton believes that teachers who ignore expressive writing make it more difficult for students to learn to write and "learn to learn."

Expressive writing is the matrix from which other forms of writing take shape. Expressive writing helps writers find out what they want to say; it is often the first stage of transactional or poetic writing. In addition, expressive writing is a unique mode of learning: thinking on paper.[3] Expressive writing is a potent learning tool for problem solving and brainstorming. Britton argues that expressive writing "may be at any stage the kind of writing best adapted to exploration and discovery. It is the language that externalizes our first stages in tackling a problem or coming to grips with an experience."[4]

Unfortunately, English teachers as well as teachers in other disciplines too often look suspiciously at expressive writing. For some it is too personal, unstructured, or informal to assign in the classroom; for others it is too difficult to evaluate; and for still others expressive writing is considered merely a remnant from the excessively liberal teaching practices of the late 1960s. Using student journals to generate expressive writing can allay such concerns, for the journal is both a rigorous assignment and, at the same time, a place for free, speculative writing.

Journal Writing

Teacher and students can use journals in class daily to write in, to read from, and to talk about—in addition to whatever private journal writing students do on their own. In-class journal writing can substitute for other routine writing assignments, from quizzes to book reports. Journal writing stimulates student discussion, starts small group activity, clarifies hazy issues, solves problems, and re-inforces learning. Journals work because every time students write entries they are individualizing their instruction; writing silently—even for five minutes—is conscious, deliberate mental *activity*. Students can't daydream, doze off, or fidget while writing—unless they write about it, and even that becomes a conscious choice. Journal writing will not make passive students miraculously active learners; but it will make it harder for them to remain passive. Try some of the following ideas.

1. Introduce a discussion class with a five-minute journal-write. Any class. Any subject. Use the journal to bridge the gap between the student's former activity (walking, eating, listening) and your classroom. Suggest a topic related to the day's lesson—a quote from the reading assignment, for instance—and ask students to use those first few minutes to compose (literally) their thoughts and to focus them in a public direction. Without such preparatory time, initial discussions are often halting and groping. Initiate the discussion by asking someone to read an entry out loud. It is hard to read rapidly-written words in public, but it is also rewarding when the language generates a response from classmates. You may sometimes wish to read your own entry first to put the class at ease, for your sentences may be awkward, halting, and fragmentary just as those of your students sometimes are. Repeated periodically, this exercise provides students with a structured oral entry into the difficult public arena of the classroom and helps affirm the value of their personal voice.

2. Precede your lecture with a short journal-write. Like the discussion class, the lecture also benefits from a transition exercise which starts students thinking about the scheduled topic. For example, prior to beginning a lecture in a nineteenth-century American literature class studying "Transcendentalism," ask students to define their concept of romanticism in writing. This brief exercise sets the scene for the lecture. Alternatively, you might use a short discussion based on the student writing as a lead into the lecture. Either way, the students have involved themselves with the material because they have committed words to paper.

3. End a class with a journal-write. Ask students to pull together information or ideas they have learned during class. Their summaries can serve several purposes: "What did you learn in here today—one thing—anything?" or "What questions are still unanswered?" These questions can be handled orally, of course, without recourse to the journal, but forcing loose thoughts onto paper

sometimes generates tighter thinking. And again, the private act of writing encourages students to collect thoughts otherwise lost in the push-and-shove hurry to leave class. Too often instructors lecture right to the bell, trying to make one last point, while at the same time realizing by the rustle in the room that the students are already mentally on their way to lunch. Better, perhaps, to cover less lecture territory and to end class with students recording their own observations and summaries. That final act of writing/thinking helps students to synthesize material for themselves, and thereby increases its value.

4. Interrupt a fifty-minute lecture with a five-minute journal-write. Listening is passive and note taking often mechanical; even the best students drift into daydreams from time to time. A journal-write offers students a chance to re-engage themselves personally with the lecture topic. Writing changes the pace of the class; it shifts the learner into a participant role and sometimes forces clarity from confusion simply by requiring that pen be put to paper. Writing clears out a little space for students to interact with the ideas thrown at them and allows them to focus problems while the stimulus is still fresh. "Reflect on the notion that Karl Marx is a philosopher rather than a scientist," or "Explain the phrase 'the medium is the message' in your own words." Planned in advance, these pauses serve as both welcome breaks and fruitful exercises.

A variation on the planned lecture pause is the spontaneous one, where the lecturer senses misunderstanding in the audience or where the lecturer loses track of an idea. While writing in journals either teacher or students may put their finger on the problem and so make the next fifteen or twenty minutes more profitable. Of course, instructors do not plan for misunderstanding; but if it occurs, the journal-write is one way out.

5. Interrupt a discussion for a journal-write. Refocus a digressive or rambling discussion by simply calling "time out" and asking students to write for a few minutes in their journals. "What are we trying to explain?" or "Restate the argument in your own words; then let's start again." Pauses in a discussion change the class pace and allow quiet, personal reflection. We all need a little time-out in some classes yet seldom find a pedagogical justification for it. In one-sided discussions, where a few students dominate and others can't participate, interrupt with a short journal-write and sometimes the situation will reverse itself, as quiet students find their voices and loud ones cool off. Such pauses can also raise student consciousness of the roles people play in class if the teacher asks

certain questions. "What is your part in this discussion?" or "Try to trace how we got from molecules to psychopaths in the last fifteen minutes" or "Why do you think Tom just said what he did?" Writing about talking provides distance by forcing us into the "spectator role" and thereby generating thoughts we didn't have before. Sometimes it helps.

6. Use the journal-write to solve problems. In a class on modern literature ask students to write about the lines in an e e cummings poem which they do *not* understand; the following day many students will have written their way to understanding. What better way to make sense out of "what if a much of a which of a wind" or "my father moved through dooms of love"? Math or science teachers might ask students to solve difficult equations by using journal-writes when they are confused. The journal can become a regular tool in any subject area to assist in problem solving, since the act of writing out the problem is, itself, a clarifying experience. Switching from number symbols to word symbols sometimes makes a difference; just as putting someone else's problem into your own words makes it *your* problem and so leads you one step further toward solution.

7. Assign journal writing as homework. Suggest that students respond to questions or ideas arising during the day's class—or preview topics in preparation for the next class. Ask students to keep a journal record of their responses to a current issue; on a given day these responses can form the basis for a more formal class discussion. Writing in a journal requires students to go one step beyond thinking vaguely about their responses—but stops short of the formal written assignment which may cause unproductive anxiety over form or style. In some disciplines, like engineering, math, or physics, homework questions may be less "open-ended" than the ones asked in liberal arts courses; but even in the most specialized fields some free, imaginative speculation helps. And when that speculation is recorded in the journal, students have a record to look at later that documents where they've been and perhaps suggests where to go next.

8. Keep journals to keep written records. Science and social science teachers might ask students to keep a "lab journal" as well as a lab notebook to record reactions to their experiments. Such an account adds a personal dimension to lab records and provides a place to make *connections* between one observation and the next. Perhaps such journal entries should be interleaved alongside the experimental data, adding the student's own thoughts about

that data. Field notes jotted in a biology notebook become an extended observation written in a "biology journal"; this entry, in turn, might well become the basis for a major research project. Personal reflections recorded in a history journal help a student to identify with, and perhaps to make sense of, the otherwise distant and confusing past. Trial hypotheses find first articulation in a social science journal; later, the most interesting of these ideas provides the impetus for further experimentation and study.

Ken Macrorie calls journals the "seedbeds" from which other, more public (transactional or poetic) kinds of writing will emerge.[5] Echoing Macrorie, Mark Hanson advocates using personal journals "to generate (both) academic and creative writings," adding that journal entries are the primary sources for educational growth, regardless of subject area.[6] In other words, the journal is both product and process, a snapshot album or, more accurately, a portfolio of 35 mm contact sheets from which only a few negatives will be printed into quality photographs. Each journal keeper rediscovers the value of the written record. Whether one finds the journal useful to recover a lost note or fact or just to wonder, "I thought that?," the documenting of individual thought is one of the essential liberal arts.

Reading Student Journals

Reading student journals keeps teachers in touch with student experiences—frustrations, anxieties, problems, joys, excitements. Teachers who understand the everyday realities—both mental and physical—of student life may be better teachers because they can tailor assignments and tests more precisely to student needs. Reading student journals humanizes teachers. But *reading* is not evaluating or grading.

Near the end of the term I ask students to prepare their journals for me to read, deleting entries too personal to share and adding page numbers and a table of contents for major entries. Also I ask the students to write entries in which they evaluate their own journals: "Which entries make the greatest impact on you now? Which seem least worth doing? What patterns do you find from entry to entry?" For some students this evaluation proves to be the clarifying activity of the term, the action which finally defines the purpose of the journal. In the words of one student: "For this entire term I was convinced I had no ideas of value in this journal. I repeated this belief in class several times. But now I find it isn't true.

I was surprised to find how little I wrote about dorm life and my family and how many times I led up to full-fledged ideas."

Some teachers insist on *not* reading student journals, arguing that they have no right to look at these private documents. It is a good point. However, there are important reasons why teachers ought to look at their students' journals—and precautions which can eliminate prying. First, for students just beginning to keep journals, a teacher's comment can help them expand their journals and make them more useful. Sometimes first journals have too many short entries; a teacher who notices this can suggest that students use at least a full page to develop an idea. Second, some students believe that if a writing assignment is not reviewed by teachers it has no worth; while there is more of a problem here than reading journals, the teacher may decide at the outset that reviewing the journals adds credibility to the assignment. Third, students feel that journals must "count for something"—as must every requirement in an academic setting: "If teachers don't look at these things how can they count 'em?"

To resolve the apparent paradox between the student's need for a private place to write and the benefit to both student and teacher of a teacher-reading, I ask students to keep their journals in a loose-leaf notebook and to use cardboard dividers to separate sections of the journal. In this way I am able to look at material dealing with my course and avoid more personal sections. And if portions of the student's commentary about a particular class would prove embarrassing, the loose-leaf format allows deletion of that entry prior to my perusal. I may ask for the pages concerning "American Literature," for example, skim them quickly, and hand them back with suggestions only to those students who are not gaining much from the experience. At the end of the course I may check the journals again and assign a credit/no credit mark. Or I may raise student grades for good journals (lots of writing) but not penalize students for mediocre ones. Such informal evaluation does not take a lot of time, but the benefits to both students and teacher are obvious.

Well used, journals can be exciting and humane educational tools. Journals keep students in the habit of writing regularly while they promote active learning and facilitate personal engagement. And they make teachers who assign them more aware of themselves and their teaching. Student journals might be the best interdisciplinary tools we possess, integrating personal with academic knowledge across the curriculum.

Notes

1. Fader argued in favor of a program called "English in Every Classroom" in *Hooked on Books* (New York: Berkeley, 1968); the student journal was a key component in his program. This essay is an extension of Fader's idea to college instruction.

2. James Britton et al., *The Development of Writing Ability (11-18)* (London: Macmillan Education, 1975).

3. See Janet Emig's work, especially *The Composing Process of Twelfth Graders*, NCTE English Research Report No. 13 (Urbana, Ill.: NCTE, 1971); and "Writing as a Mode of Learning," *College Composition and Communication* 28 (May 1977): 122-27.

4. Britton et al., p. 165.

5. Ken Macrorie, *Writing to Read* (Rochelle Park, N.J.: Hayden Book, 1976).

6. Mark Hanson, *Sources* (Lakeside, Cal.: INTERACT, 1978).

Increasing Writing without Increasing Grading

Patricia I. Mahieu
The Ohio State University

Elizabeth McCray
Jersey Elementary School, Alexandria, Ohio

Teachers should use every idea conceivable for getting kids to write for the sheer pleasure of writing. Most of the time the enthusiasm in an elementary or middle school classroom is directly proportionate to the teacher's own enthusiasm (or lack of it), so the well-presented ideas often find a welcome reception. Add to your enthusiasm a respect for the personality differences among classes and individuals; the writing response might surprise you.

Journals

Don't expect every child in your room to be a natural John-Boy Walton, carrying his notebook under his arm from room to room while his brain bulges with ideas screaming to be recorded. Don't despair if your students don't scramble to their desks each morning to jot down the latest incident on the bus. Do encourage everyone to keep a log of comical, unusual, or interesting happenings in class, on the playground, or at home. Do remind students that it's easy to write about something that really happened or something you saw with your own eyes or did with your own hands. This type of writing is best evaluated informally; perhaps simply by keeping a record of who is writing, how many pages, and with what regularity.

Books

Writing books is another way to increase and enrich the writing experiences of young people. All ability levels can participate. If the "low" group cannot yet compose a fictional story, perhaps they can write a nonfictional account about some favorite topic: "How Are Skyscrapers Made?" or "How to Collect Rocks." Could they write autobiographies? Could they produce picture books with three or four sentences on each page written for first- or second-graders to read? The books need not be graded and can also be created as group projects with the teacher serving only as a consultant.

Poetry

Another supplement to composition is poetry. Children enjoy poetry and are amazingly successful with many forms of it. They enjoy counting out the beats to *haiku, cinquain,* and *tanka* rhythms. They chuckle at limericks, and welcome a chance to illustrate these "easy" assignments. Poetry is fun to read and a pleasure to evaluate; poems do not require long hours with a grading pencil. A lively tonic of poetry once a month can cure the writing blahs and can provide a welcome relief from formal grading.

Class Books

The "class book" is a non-graded and completely voluntary activity. Keep a blank composition book in the classroom. Once each month begin a new story in the book. Provide a title, a setting, a description of the characters; sometimes give the first page of dialogue between two characters, or insert a drawing, a photograph, or a picture from a magazine. After the book has been introduced to the class, invite all the students to participate in the writing of the story. This activity could result, for example, in the continuing saga of "The Incredible Bulk."

Pen Pals

Another way to increase writing and to decrease the paper load is to find a pen pal for every student in the class. The pen pal can be as far away as another country or as close as the room across the hall. Pen pals can write to each other weekly or monthly. They can exchange letters, poems, stories, jokes, and ideas. Most students quickly respond to the idea of tidying up a paper if someone they care for is going to read it. The evaluation of this kind of writing is ensured: Did your pen pal write back to you?

Writing Plays

The writing of a play is particularly suited to small-group authorship. Short plays can later be staged, taped as radio plays, or produced as puppet plays. The evaluation for this activity is realized when the audience responds to the finished product.

Class Newspaper

A classroom newspaper can provide an opportunity for practicing many forms of writing as well as other language arts skills. Students can be divided into small committees, each concerned with one aspect of the newspaper. The sports, editorial, news, entertainment, society, and classified sections of the paper must be written, proofread, and assembled onto dummy sheets; students can type and print the paper themselves. The evaluation occurs when the paper comes off the press and is distributed to the readers. Is it interesting, readable, grammatically correct? Are the students satisfied with the effort and do they have suggestions for improvements? This project is an excellent assignment for a teacher's aide or a volunteer parent or grandparent.

Class Yearbook

Toward the end of the school year your class might want to assemble individual personality profiles or mini-autobiographies into a giant "Class of '79" yearbook. Each student can write pertinent facts about his or her own personality, hobbies, skills, family. Interesting anecdotes, favorite subjects, descriptions of projects or activities especially liked or disliked can also be included. This book can be illustrated as well with Polaroid pictures or drawings. Carefully bound and prominently displayed in next year's writing center, this album can be loads of fun for aspiring young authors and may serve as an effective September motivator. Again, no formal evaluation is required, but the benefits of the project are obvious.

Teachers should provide a variety of opportunities and incentives for writing, and the completed work should be displayed.

The displayed work is evaluated by the students themselves as they gather to read the most recently posted writings. Students can learn to enjoy writing for pleasure, and grading these kinds of papers is unnecessary and ill-advised.

Try everything!—but don't try to *grade* everything. Give your students many opportunities for meaningful writing, and grade enough of their work to enable you to make a fair evaluation of their ability and progress. Realize that the key to learning is doing; your grading pencil is not your most valuable tool, your imagination is. There are legitimate ways to reduce the paper load and still enhance the language arts instruction in your classroom.

2 Teacher Involvement—Not Evaluation

Get Involved in the Writing Process: Do Yourself and Your Students a Favor

Nancy L. Roser
The University of Texas at Austin

Julie M. Jensen
The University of Texas at Austin

Room 103

Betty Danner moved quickly around her classroom, making certain once again that each of her twenty-four third graders had pencil and paper before she launched the weekly "creative writing" assignment. Sometimes, Betty mused, it seemed that Fridays and writing rolled around almost before the papers from the week before had been marked and returned. Some of the children had *so* many problems with composing complete thoughts, with spelling, with using capitals.

"What are we supposed to write about, Ms. Danner?" The small voice shook her from her reverie to an immediate reply: "It's a hot, hot summer day and you should write how you would feel if you were an ice cream cone."

As was the custom on writing day, the children bent over their papers and Ms. Danner returned to her desk to grade the workbooks. The only sounds to be heard were the scratches of pencils and an occasional word spelled aloud.

That evening Betty Danner faced the stack of compositions, bolstered by a pillow and a TV movie.

Room 204

Pat Clover took the wriggling rabbit from the gentle hands of the last first grader. "And what might a rabbit like this want for its name?" she asked, and smiled at the deluge of offerings. The visiting cottontail had certainly sparked some lively conversation in her room, as well as several interesting questions and vivid descriptions. She had heard words like "powdery soft" and "rippling ears." Besides the descriptions, Ms. Clover had encouraged the children to speculate on facts (e.g., where the bunny had been born, what it ate), to learn vocabulary (e.g., "What do you call a rabbit's home?" and "What is another name for a rabbit?"), and to stretch their imaginations (e.g., "How might you feel if you were Hopper visiting your first school and your first class of first graders?" or "What might this rabbit say if it could talk?").

It was the children who suggested that stories about the rabbit's visit comprise the newest addition to a collection of books based upon classroom experiences. A group of children went smoothly into action: two passed paper, allowing their classmates to select the number of sheets they wanted and also to choose from among various paper sizes, shapes, and colors; one passed a basket containing a variety of writing instruments; a third moved the rabbit's wire cage to a place where all the authors could see it as they wrote.

Ms. Clover moved around the room, chatting quietly with the writers who stopped her, listening as they read their words to her or softly reading them aloud, and responding to the content: "I'm glad you decided to describe our rabbit's tail. What else could we say to make sure everyone who reads our book knows exactly what Hopper looks like?" Or: "I think a bunny like Hopper might feel just as you wrote, Randy. Why, to have all these big, strange eyes on you and to be so small! What else do you plan to write about Hopper?"

When she was asked, Ms. Clover wrote difficult words on a small pad, then tore off the sheet, leaving the word for the writer, and moved on. Later these words were added to a personal dictionary.

Now more children attempt to spell for themselves in this classroom, both because it is encouraged and because they write often and feel comfortable with the process. Ms. Clover never responds to a request for a word with an admonishment or a phonics lesson: "Try to sound it out." Instead, she supplies the word and retains a focus on content: "Here it is. What an interesting word you want! How are you using it?" At other times, when the writer's ideas are flowing, she merely slips the word beside the child's paper and moves on.

During the twenty to twenty-five minutes the children are writing, Ms. Clover typically reads, leads, and confers with all of them. Many who were extremely dependent on her a few weeks before are increasingly in control, probably because they write daily and are encouraged by their teacher and by pride in their work.

In the evening, Ms. Clover catches her favorite television show without a stack of papers in her lap. She is instead thinking of enriching experiences from which future writing will spring. The papers are at school—unfinished. They await the finishing touches a writer must apply before inviting a reader to share the completed, bound, bunny-shaped book.

Reducing Teacher Homework
Increasing Teacher Schoolwork

It is evident that of the two teachers described, Ms. Clover faces the greater amount of student writing, offers children more and richer writing opportunities, and provides for more encounters with blank paper. But Ms. Danner, ironically, has the bigger stack of homework, the largest paperload. Let's examine the assumptions upon which each teacher conducts her writing program to determine how these scenarios reveal teacher values, demands on children, and use of student-teacher time.

Teacher Values

Both teachers seem to value a time set aside for writing, but Ms. Danner plans fewer opportunities to write. We have seen that one reason for infrequent writing is the time required for reading and marking student efforts. Other reasons may be just as valid: (1) The teacher may run short of story starters or "creative" writing assignments; (2) The students may respond negatively to writing: "I don't know what to write"; or (3) Students may show so many writing problems that it becomes easier to assign mimeographed practice sheets that focus on specific error patterns than to provide blank paper that allows the problem floodgates to swing fully open. Whatever the specific reasons, the situation in Ms. Danner's classroom seems to reflect the values of a teacher who believes: (1) that writing is so unnatural an event that it must always be scheduled and artificially induced; (2) that the goal of writing instruction is a "mistake-free" product which is achieved through the at-home "correcting" of student papers; and (3) that learning to write is best accomplished in skill increments or through carefully sequenced writing tasks, rather than through the holistic expression of thought and experience.

Ms. Clover's writing values and objectives appear to be somewhat different. She seems to believe: (1) that writing will not occur in a vacuum—mental, experiential, or environmental; (2) that both experiences and talk about experiences feed thought and are prerequisite to fluent written expression; and (3) that written products evolve gradually through a multi-stage process beginning with a search for ideas to be shared, progressing to a crude written representation of those ideas, and concluding with refinements dictated by the purposes of the writer.

Perhaps an oversimplified comparison is this: Ms. Danner, and teachers like her, value only the written product and so they work with it; Ms. Clover, and teachers like her, value the writing process as well and view it as a significant part of their instructional role.

Demands on Children

The writing tasks of Ms. Danner and Ms. Clover placed different demands on the students. Our product-oriented teacher Ms. Danner asked students to write on a topic removed from their experiences; then she retreated to her desk, conveying an attitude of "you" (the student writers) and "me" (the non-writing teacher), instead of "we/us" (a team working toward improved writing). Finally, she viewed her role as after-the-fact *evaluator* of "finished" written products rather than as *responder* to children in the act of writing.

The child's awareness of a teacher's forthcoming judgment of the product may result in the subordination of experimentation with ideas to an excessive concern with mechanical perfection: "What is that rule for the spelling of *believe*? I guess I'll just use *think*." "How will I include that joke the tour guide told us when I don't remember where the quotation marks go? I'd better play it safe and just summarize."

Teachers like Ms. Clover who value the process of writing recognize the importance of nurturing ideas to be expressed. They communicate a "writer at the controls" attitude to their students, viewing themselves as questioners, extenders, and listeners to children in the *act* of writing with a sense of authority about their own experiences. They value the development of self-critical skills and lead children to identify specific strengths in their writing and to set precise and personal writing goals. Their students tap peers and teacher as resources, from the time of early efforts toward the clarification of their ideas to later steps which assure that their writing is in a standard form, ready for an audience. These students share with their teacher and peers a delight in just the right word and in an imaginative idea. They are members of a team of writers—which includes the teacher. They are spared the frustrations of the cycle: write about "My Summer Vacation"—turn in the paper to the teacher—receive corrections and a grade—recopy—write about "What I'd Do with a Million Dollars," etc.

Student-Teacher Time

Ms. Danner chose to offer a writing "stimulus" and then to sit out the classroom time set aside for writing, serving occasionally as a spelling consultant. The bulk of her time investment occurred later—with paper, not with children. The emphasis upon reacting to writing separated her in time and space from the author.

Ms. Clover believes that the teacher's time is best spent in planning and preparing experiences that will stimulate language and therefore enrich writing. She uses her time to respond to writing when writing is happening; she encourages growth through frequent, usually brief, teacher-student encounters over the flowing written words. Ms. Clover values the time she spends interacting with the writers because of what she learns about them as writers: their strengths and needs, their styles in approaching the writing task, the extent of their commitment to writing, among other things. Whatever Ms. Clover learns while children write helps her to help children grow as writers.

Read the Papers in Class

Thomas Newkirk
University of New Hampshire

The first article appearing in *The English Journal*, written by Edwin Hopkins and published in 1912, was entitled "Can Good Composition Teaching Be Done Under Present Conditions?" It begins:

> No.
> This is a small and apparently unprotected word, occupying a somewhat exposed position; but it is upborne by indisputable truth.
> If another answer were possible, if good teaching can be done under present conditions, it is passing strange that so few teachers have found out how to do it; that English composition teachers as a class, if judged by criticism that is becoming more and more frequent, are so abnormally inefficient .... Every year teachers resign, break down, perhaps become permanently invalided, having sacrificed ambition, health, and in not a few instances even life, in the struggle to do all the work expected of them.

One reads Hopkins's article with the eerie feeling that absolutely nothing has changed. The reasons Hopkins gives are too familiar. At that time there had been a shift from the dry-bones teaching of rhetoric to the principle that "pupils should learn to write by writing." In the terminology of the day, English composition had become a laboratory subject. Yet secondary schools made no attempt to add personnel to handle the increased workload of teachers, and the average pupil load remained 128, about what it is today. The solution, according to Hopkins, was to reduce this number to 80.

I suspect Hopkins's plea had little effect; his despairing tone suggests as much. I also suspect that current pleas for smaller classes will have little effect, given the tax-cutting mood of the country. English teachers will continue to be faced with rising public expectations without a corresponding increase in support. Can good composition teaching be done under these conditions?

Yes.

This is a small and somewhat unprotected word, but it is borne out by the work of a number of English teachers who must deal with the traditionally heavy secondary school workload. Ironically, the key to handling this load is the concept of laboratory that Hopkins uses. In the laboratory the teacher assists students who are in the process of conducting experiments; the teacher advises, questions, evaluates, and helps with individual problems. The laboratory setting obliges the teacher to enter into the students' work as it is going on, recognizing that more learning can occur through the two-way communication. The laboratory teacher also leaves school at the end of the day, relatively unburdened, with no piles of papers to grade.

Maybe the laboratory teacher has something, though. Why can't the English teacher read and respond to papers in class? I've never met an English teacher who couldn't talk faster than he could write. I've never met English students who didn't prefer a brief oral explanation of a problem to "awk" and "agr" penciled in the margin of their papers. (I've never met a student who really understood what "awk" and "agr" meant.) I've never met a teacher who enjoyed writing meticulous comments on a paper only to watch the student look at the grade and then file the paper in a notebook—or a trashcan.

A teacher who wants to move toward the laboratory approach must make some changes in the way classes are run. While the teacher meets with individual students, the class should be working independently—writing, reading, reading each other's writing. Since students will be graded on their best work, they should be encouraged to revise and perfect a piece of writing or abandon it if it is going nowhere. Probably the most crucial change is the need for the teacher to learn to read papers quickly and to respond in a way that helps students revise their work.

Amazingly little has been written on reading student writing, and those articles that do deal with the subject seem to make two questionable assumptions. The first is that reading a paper is synonymous with making a final evaluation of it. And the second is that the real problem with reading student papers is establishing criteria for "good writing."

As long as teachers don't involve themselves in the writing process, there is no reason to see reading as anything more than making a final evaluation. We assign the paper; they write it; we grade it. But a teacher who reads progressive drafts, reads for different reasons at different stages of the process. Such a teacher will not offer counsel on the correct use of the semicolon when the student is groping for a focus. Donald Murray writes:

> The experienced composition teacher does not see all writing problems—spelling and structure and lack of subject matter—of equal importance. He encourages the student to see that on most pieces of writing there is one fundamental problem that must be dealt with before the next problem can be spotted and then solved. For example, an incoherent paper will be ungrammatical; once the logic of the paper is developed, grammatical problems tend to disappear.[1]

The second assumption, that the major problem with reading papers is defining a set of criteria, implies that the major problem is one of values when in fact it is often one of reading behavior. The fact that teachers have agreed on how much to weigh "content" does not guarantee that all teachers will see the "content" in a paper. Teachers read papers differently, process the print differently, and often unconsciously adopt different strategies. I'm not arguing for a uniform method of reading, one which would eliminate differences in evaluation (which would be impossible, boring, unhealthy), but I am suggesting that writing teachers become consciously aware of their reading strategies, that they should learn to be disciplined readers.

If studies of the reading process tell us anything, they tell of the primacy of purpose. Reading is not simply decoding—transferring print into sound; it is a process of fulfilling purposes, of raising questions to be answered. Russell Stauffer writes:

> Regulating reading by purposes—by questions to be answered— sets up a perplexity that demands a solution. This need to resolve a perplexity steadies and guides the reader-thinker, and controls the rate and type of reading undertaken. In other words, the nature of the purposes to be achieved fixes the answers to be sought, and regulates the rate and scope of the reading-thinking process.[2]

So what happens when a teacher reads a paper? Too often there is a confusion of aims; the teacher throws out a big net to see what he or she can catch, reading for content, focus, style, and mechanics simultaneously. By trying to read at a number of levels, the teacher does not read effectively at any. In pausing to correct mechanical errors, he or she is distracted from the meaningful content and possibilities of the paper. At the same time, the meaning of the paper often carried the teacher over mechanical errors; those that are marked are marked sporadically.

The writing teacher needs to define a sequence of purposes that will both match the progression of the writing process and will steady the teacher's own reading process. The following model is based on the classical view of the composing process (excluding memory and delivery): *inventio* (invention or the discovery of ideas and arguments), *dispositio* (arrangement), and *elocutio* (style or language). For each stage I offer the major questions I ask as I read.

Reading for Discovery. The major weakness in student writing is not, as newspapers would have us believe, an inability to write sentences, to punctuate accurately, or even to spell correctly. The major weakness is underdevelopment, writing that is information-thin, detail-thin. This lack of development is due in part to egocentrism, to the inability of students to internalize the viewpoint of a reader. Details, reasons, background information, logical connections that are self-evident to them are often not self-evident to the reader.

A second reason for underdevelopment is the failure of student writers to compensate for the slowness of the physical act of writing. They find it difficult to remember that a laboriously written paragraph will occupy the reader for only a few seconds. This disparity often causes students to overestimate the amount of information they have included. Finally, young writers lack self-confidence. One eleventh grade writer, when asked what allowances she made for her audience, responded, "I usually give less detail and more vague descriptions for the audience so I won't bore them." Such writers fail to understand that it is precisely this lack of detail that will bore the reader. They need to be assured that people are indeed nosy, that they love detail.

The underdeveloped paper presents the teacher with an interesting problem. The teacher must read for what isn't there, for that which is only suggested. Often the clue is an adjective—"beautiful," "frightening," "unbelievable"—that suggests a general impression that must be supported by detail. Sometimes there is a change in tone or voice that indicates the writer has discovered his subject. Peter Elbow's term for this kind of reader reaction, "center of gravity" response, is a good one, for it implies an almost physical response to an initial draft, the sense of being drawn in at a point in the reading.

The teacher reads a first draft with a benevolent tentativeness, looking for possibilities, for opportunities implicit in the piece. Often the revision of a paper will be only marginally related to the original draft; for example, by writing about summer at Grandfather's farm, the student realizes that he really wants to write about Grandfather.

I have found the following questions useful when reading for discovery.

1. What is working?
2. At what points does the paper need more detail?
3. At what points does the paper need further documentation?
4. Is the paper sufficiently complex? Are important alternatives explored? Are important questions answered?
5. Is the paper focused? Does it seem to make one point, create one dominant impression?

The first question is the most important and one that teachers, in their zeal to improve a paper, tend to forget. But students learn more by being shown what they are doing well than by being shown what they are doing poorly. If the teacher focuses exclusively on problems, the student gets the unintended message that he or she has done a poor job.

In developing these questions I tried to determine if a concern for information and detail preceded a concern for focus. I have concluded that the relationship is not linear but cyclical. The student moves toward a topic because of a vaguely defined (though often strong) interest or emotional attachment. As the student gathers information, he or she refines this initial attachment into a focus; as the student refines the focus, a clearer idea of the information needed develops. In an initial reading I try to break into this cycle. Consider, for example, the following first draft by an eleventh grader:

> I have always seemed to look upon my mother as someone very special. She is special because she is a friend.
> I admire her firmness in what she believes. Although I am spoiled she will not give into a request if she is against it. I may look down on her at times, but I realize its hard on her too.
> My mother has had a very hard life and sometimes I do not understand how she can take the pressure any longer. When she gets really upset we talk and I try to understand.
> I admire my mother because she is full of pride. Her pride stands in the way sometimes, but I have no complaints.
> If my friends have a bad reputation she will not look down on them until they do something to lose her respect. She will give anyone a chance and that is something to be admired in someone who has not been given a chance.

While there are a number of ways to respond to this piece, I feel the pull—the center of gravity response—when I come to the last sentence. There she seems to have found a focus. I would ask how this thesis could generate information. What details could be added to show her mother has not been given a chance? What details could show her openness and tolerance?

Reading for Arrangement. Once the student has discovered a focus and located the necessary information, the teacher needs to read for arrangement. I find a new set of questions helpful for reading for arrangement.

1. What has been improved?
2. Does the beginning begin the piece?
3. Does the ending end it?
4. Is the information presented in a clear order? Are transitions between paragraphs clear?
5. Are there any weak sections that can be eliminated?

Again the first task of the reader is to find something that works, to acknowledge improvements that have been made. The second question relates to the common tendency of young (and not so young) writers to "clear the throat" before getting to the subject. A paper on skiing does not begin on the top of the slopes; the writer must tell us when he woke up and what he ate for breakfast and what route he took to get to Pleasant Valley. Or, in an expository paper on repairing cars, the writer must inform us that automotive travel is an important aspect (always an "aspect") of American society.

Padded endings are also common. The writer feels compelled to tell us what he's told us. The writer ends an exciting account of the ascent of Mount Washington with a flaccid paragraph to the effect that the climb truly was a learning experience. William Zinnser's advice is helpful here: "When you're ready to stop, stop. If you have presented all the facts and made the point you want to make, look for the nearest exit." Questions two and three overlap question five. As I see it, only on the second reading should the teacher worry about what might be cut. A bush must be overgrown before it can be pruned.

Reading for Style and Language. At this stage the reading is slow, even tedious, because the teacher is no longer concerned with meaning but with sentence structure and mechanics. There is a shift from meaning to code. This type of reading takes place near the end of a marking period. By this time students have invested a great deal of time in their papers and are therefore motivated to take the final step. It is *not* the teacher's job to become the student's copyreader, responsible for locating every error. Rather, the teacher should read a sample of the student's work, no more than 500 words. If the student has basic problems in sentence structure or mechanics, they are likely to appear on this sample. Once the teacher has explained the difficulties in the sample, it is the student's job to complete the editing.

Here are the questions I use when reading for language and style.

1. When possible, has the student used the subject-verb-object sentence thus avoiding the wordiness of the passive voice and the sentences beginning "there is," "there are," etc.?

2. Are there sentences that could be profitably combined?

3. Can the writer eliminate unnecessary words, particularly adverbs?

4. Is the movement from sentence to sentence clear?

5. What types of spelling errors is the writer making?

6. Are the sentence boundaries correctly marked?

7. Has the writer violated the rules of usage or mechanics in a way that draws attention away from content?

This list could go on, but it shouldn't. Even during this final reading, the teacher should be selective. Too often writing teachers look for errors with the zeal of bounty hunters. The goal, however, should not be the detection of a number of errors but the diagnosis of a major type of error. Such a disciplined approach suggests to the student that problems with sentence structure and mechanics are manageable.

I realize that by listing questions for each level of reading, I may have given the impression that the teacher must give a detailed response to each paper. Not so. For any one reading of any one paper, the teacher will probably be dealing with only one or two questions in a conference that lasts no more than four minutes.

Even so it's hard work. At times the teacher, moving from student to student, will feel like one of the jugglers on the old Ed Sullivan Show, the ones who would balance twenty plates on the top of spinning sticks. They would move frantically from stick to stick, spinning and respinning so the plates would not crash. The writing class I am describing is only slightly less frantic. But at the end of the day the writing teacher can leave the building unburdened, arms swinging freely.

Notes

1. Donald Murray, "Finding Your Own Voice: Teaching Composition in an Age of Dissent," *College Composition and Communication* 20 (May, 1969): 122.
2. Russell G. Stauffer, *Directed Reading Maturity as a Cognitive Process* (New York: Harper and Row, 1969), p. 26.

Role Playing, Writing, and Red Pencils

Monica L. Josten
South Milwaukee Junior High

Ordinarily, paper load is not a problem in remedial junior high classes. Oh, teachers devise many a make-shift assignment. But who does any work in a "low ability" section?

"Hey, teacher, we don't do no work in here."

"This is the mental class. Don't ya even know that?"

"Boy, is she dumb."

"Another bummer. Shiiiiit. We always get the bummers."

Obviously, this is not the time for a lecture on the fascinations lurking beneath the course title, Remedial Ninth Grade English. Having confronted the ninth grade "bad guys" with almost seasonal regularity for the past nine years, it takes a lot more than the first day loud-mouths to discourage me. I stand back, listen, watch, judge. At least, in a class like this my work is clear-cut.

Somehow, under my direction we must learn to get along with each other. I will try to approach each of these "characters" as an intelligent human being who has an inherent capacity and a right to learn to read and to write well enough to function in a highly technological society. And what about them? Do they have obligations, too? Eventually these young people must come to understand their role as free citizens in a skill-intensive working environment; and finally, they must be willing to assume the responsibility for their own learning.

This task no longer appalls or disheartens me. I think to myself, I've seen harder shells than these split wide open in a year's time. Besides, I know that I have caused this uproar by handing out blank sheets of paper and offering to "lend" a pencil to anyone who has arrived *sans* scholarly instrument.

When the uproar quiets down, I ignore the paper and pencils on each desk and say, "I want to tell a story."

"Is it true?"

"I don't know."

"Who's it about?"

"Me."

"If it's about you, how come you don-know if it's true."

"Told ya she was dumb."

"Be quiet so I can tell my story. Now. I'm a middle-aged lady . . ."

Nods of agreement.

". . . who lives in one of these houses here around the junior high . . ."

"Why do ya drive yer car to work if ya live so close?"

I, of course, am role playing, but they have not realized this yet. By the time they do realize it, they will be fully into their roles.

". . . and I have three kids . . ."

"Boy, do I feel sorry for them kids."

". . . but they're too young for junior high, so they go to the grade school across the playing field. Anyway, every day at lunch time, junior high kids pass by my house. They cut across my lawn. They break down my bushes and ruin my flower garden. They toss apple cores and sandwich chunks on my grass. They scare my little kids."

"And throw stuff at yer car?"

"Yes, they do that, too." Now we are all listening because we recognize a familiar, even daily, occurrence around our school.

I continue, "Finally, I get really mad; so I write a letter to the local newspaper demanding that the junior high school shorten the lunch hour to twenty minutes and keep the kids in during the lunch time."

"No."

"I won't stay in."

"You . . . you . . ."

I begin to talk louder, faster. "I can't see any reason why kids have to go out at noontime. School is for studying, and I think kids should be inside doing school work."

Protestations are becoming vituperative, but I am undaunted.

"A school board member reads my letter. He invites me and my neighbors to come to a special meeting to voice our complaints. At this meeting the members of the school board will decide whether or not to close the junior high at lunch time."

Someone shakes a fist at me. Others merely shout insults.

I clap both hands over my ears and announce, "I'm not listening. Write your answers."

Trapped. Mouths hang open. Eyes look at me. My ears are still covered. "Write to the school board members. Prove to them that I'm wrong."

Hesitantly, pencils meet paper. The hands are unskilled. The letters are malformed and the words scrawling. Punctuation is erratic and spelling, at best, atrocious. But writing is taking place. Someone tries to speak. Again, covering my ears, I refuse to listen; I do not speak. At this time, the medium of communication is the written word. I see frustration, anger, scratching out, pounding on desks. I remain totally unresponsive. Eventually, everyone settles down to some attempt at writing. Except for an occasional snort, shuffle, "aha," or foot stomp, the room is quiet. When each one seems engrossed in expounding before the school board my colossal doltishness, I call out, "Time."

"What?" The speaker looks annoyed.

"Time." I act as nonchalant as possible. "Time to stop writing."

"Stop? I just got started."

"I can't stop. I'm not finished."

"Don't pay any attention ta her. Jist keep writin'."

"What'd I say? She really is dumb."

Forced into acquiescence, I grant more time. My ruse is working. Imagine the ninth-grade "bad guys" maneuvered into a position where they demand from the teacher more time for writing. After a decent interval, we all decide to halt the pencils. I walk down the rows, picking up the papers. A satisfied grunt greets me as I lift a paper from a desk. Back in front of the room, I quickly glance through the papers, arranging them in an order suitable to my purpose. The very act of shuffling through papers returns me to the role of teacher, and I feel immediately not the hot anger toward the enraged neighbor lady but the apathetic hostility reserved for school authorities.

I hold the assembled papers in one hand. "This is the *Voice Journal.* All your letters have been printed in the local newspaper."

Guffaws.

"Yes. The editor printed them." I'm the neighbor lady again. "The newspaper with your letters comes to my house the day of the school board meeting."

A few eyes widen. These kids are in remedial English, but they are not stupid people.

"That evening I take the newspaper along when I go, together with my neighbors, to complain before the school board."

"Oh-oh."

I walk to the classroom door and reenter, waving the "newspaper" in my hand. The front blackboard serves as a silent but foreboding school board. Brandishing my papers, I march before the board, read in irate tones, "dumb old lady," "her stupid kids," "who cares about her grass," "we won't stay in even if you tell us." I reserve for the last a hate-filled utterance that threatens, "I'd like to meet her in a dark alley some night and I hope I have my knife."

Imitating the shrill screams of a frightened suburban matron, I shout, "See, I told you they were irresponsible. The streets aren't safe with them out there. Lock 'em up."

Silence. No one speaks or even moves. I turn around to face my class again. I do not speak.

Someone says, "Well, what now? Are they gonna close the lunch hour?"

"Ya know they will," a dejected voice.

Even my old friend, pensively, "We were really dumb."

"Ya."

"But it wasn't a real letter, was it? We could just throw those away; and we could write new letters, couldn't we?"

I smile, an open friendly smile.

A voice asks, "Did you really write that letter? Are you really gonna go to the school board?"

I shrug.

"Naaa," another voice, "she jist said that ta make us write, didn't ya?"

I wink.

"That was a pritty good trick," my old friend. "Ya, a pritty good trick . . ."

". . . for a dumb teacher." I finish his sentence for him.

Tomorrow we will write to the school board again. This time we'll be more clever. Before we start writing, I'll give a few hints about composing a letter of complaint or protest—the very hints they would have scoffed at today. They would have disrupted my "lesson" on a "letter of complaint" and then refused to write the letter. But tomorrow they will write, all of them.

What about me, though? What role do I play once the papers start coming in? Certainly, not the role of paper corrector. Shall I take these papers, correct every spelling error, rearrange the awkward sentences, try to insert basic punctuation? How can I? From my point of view, this task would take forever. And what will it be worth? These kids have been red penciled into refusing to turn in any papers. That's why they're in remedial English. Obviously, however, I ought not encourage them to write without some formal attempt to improve their skill.

My writing program relies on role playing, short writing samples, and on-the-spot corrections. The program makes the teacher's red pencil a *verboten* instrument.

All writing is done in class. It is always on a specifically assigned topic. At this stage, remedial students are not capable of initiating their own writing subjects. Unless the topic is very clear, they will become frustrated, disruptive, and waste the entire period. The allotted time for writing is best kept short and only gradually increased as confidence, skill, and willingness to write develop.

While the students write, I walk about the room, looking over shoulders, giving encouragement, making on-the-spot corrections. These on-the-spot corrections are the only direct corrections I will make. In offering suggestions for better writing, I never take over the pencil and put marks on a student's paper. Apparently, such marks are an insufferable indignity that brings forth rebellion in remedial students. Precisely why this is true I do not know, but I try to respect the feeling. If it is necessary to show the formation of a letter or the spelling of a word, scrap paper serves as an inoffensive medium of improvement.

Of course, in a remedial English class, there is never a time when the students work quietly at improving their writing while the teacher performs some totally unconnected task at his or her desk. Any such show of unconcerned detachment is sure to produce zinging spitballs, flying erasers, and punching fists.

A more indirect, but not less effective, method of correction involves a role playing scenario. Immediately after the papers have been collected, I set the stage, usually through a story. The imaginary scene must represent a real-life situation in which writing of the type just handed in would normally be read. I play the person who would read such news articles, letters of application, or business requests. In an officious manner, I set about my task of reading aloud each piece of writing.

If a particular piece is very badly written, I will read an extemporaneously corrected version so as not to embarrass the student writer into refusing to write again. Because the students have just handed in their papers, they remember what they have written. They know that what I am reading is not the same. This is an effective but nondiscouraging method of telling young persons they have a long way to travel yet on the writing line.

These role playing reading sessions are most effective when students play themselves. Although the writers are themselves, I am no longer the teacher. Now their work is being judged not as a class assignment but as a response to a real-life situation. Remedial students will take corrections from "real" people that they will not take from teachers.

Many times I have tried to reason with myself why these remedial students feel so alienated from, even hostile to, anything connected with school—teachers, assignments, rules, corrections. In observing their behavior, listening to their conversations, I detect a sense of the "unreal" about school. They consider school an entity totally detached from the real life they experience. To them, an English composition assignment is just that, a composition assignment, and no more. They do not understand that the school composition is an exercise developed to sharpen their skill for real-life writing tasks. Since they see no connection between real life and school compositions, the conscientious teacher's corrections have no meaning for them; and the red marked papers only reinforce their already entrenched belief that school isn't their kind of life anyway.

In my classroom, the role playing and composition reading sessions are an attempt to connect writing skills and real-life situations. Until these remedial students comprehend that writing is a form of real-life communication, they will refuse to write. Forgetting for a moment that I am an English teacher and considering myself solely as an educated human being, I know that I learned to write by writing. I did not learn to write because some former teacher assiduously red-penciled my spelling errors. I expect the same is true of my students, remedial to accelerated. Once those papers come rolling in, the quality of their writing will improve even though my red pencil lies buried beneath the gum wads in the classroom trash basket.

Learn by Doing: A Writer's Approach to Reading

Lucy McCormick Calkins
University of New Hampshire

The children in my elementary classroom write, then read what they have written, rewrite, then reread. Pushing ahead, then pulling back, the processes of reading and writing work together. Word by word, page by page, the writers move between writing and reading as they build and shape and discover their meaning. Ciardi describes this sequence when he says, "The last act of writing must be to become one's own reader. It is, I suppose, a schizophrenic process. To begin passionately and to end critically, to begin hot and to end cold; and, more important, to try to be passion-hot and critic-cold at the same time."

When Eric finishes "My Trip to the Amish Country," he steps back to see what he has written. He reads his own words and asks, "What have I said? What is my point?" I am reminded of Michener who says, "You write the first draft to see how it is going to come out."

The questions lead Eric to redefine his subject, to limit his topic. He writes a second draft, this time focusing only on the bunk beds on the train. Eric still describes the Amish countryside, but this time he describes it as seen from his bunk bed. He writes, "Out my window I could see Amish boys mowing the grass and men in dark suits on their way to church . . . ."

Now that Eric has established a focus, he again views his paper with the critical eye of a reader. He reconsiders each paragraph and each sentence to be sure they carry his reader toward his main point. He moves between reading and writing, between pushing ahead and pulling back, as line by line he builds his main point.

Eric knows he is learning to write toward a focus. What he doesn't realize is that he is also developing a sophisticated ability to read for the main idea.

Children who read and rewrite what they have written can become aware of the structure as well as the subject of writing. Writers must be architects. My children spend much of Monday morning charting and drawing and trying out designs for their writing. Geoff explores his options for a paper about his new trombone by writing ten different lead sentences. Each new opening suggests another plan, a new design. Andrea lists and numbers details she has collected for a paper about bringing home her report card. Dougie draws a war scene. Then he looks at what he has drawn, shows it to a friend, and they choose one explosion to draw in detail and to write about.

Other children explore possible designs for their writing by making exploratory drafts. They reread and reconsider the direction of each, and choose one to develop. Laura found she could tell about falling on the ice from a variety of perspectives. She could approach her topic from any time perspective she chose; she didn't have to write "first things first." These are two alternatives she liked:

> My head throbbed. I lay still on the cold ice. Minutes clicked by before I climbed onto my feet and began skating again. The whirling in my head went away, I skated for hours.
> Later, when I was home, I reached up to touch the bump on my head. Then I saw my hand was covered with warm, gushing blood. . . .

> I gingerly reach up and touch the bump I'd gotten earlier when I fell on the ice. It still felt sore. I glanced down at my hand. It was covered with warm thick blood. I raced to the bathroom mirror. There was blood caked to my hair, dried to my neck.

> Laura Poole
> Age 9

Laura decided to begin her writing with discovering blood on her hands. When she finished this draft, she pulled away and viewed it as a reader, as an outsider. She saw the strained connections in her sequence, the holes in her logic. Laura read and reread her piece as she tried to build and rebuild a sequence which would work. She learned to read—and to write—with an eye to the organization of the main idea, to the shape of the subject.

Children who write will also learn to read with an ear. All good writers are part poet. They listen to what they write. Over and

over, they read their sentences outloud. Zinsser makes this point
in his book, *On Writing Well*:

> If all your sentences move at the same plodding gait, which
> even you recognize as deadly but you don't know how to cure
> them, read them outloud. You will begin to hear where the
> trouble lies. See if you can gain variety by reversing the order of
> a sentence, by substituting a word that has freshness or oddity.

When Andrea read the beginning of her draft, "Being Mad," this
is what she heard:

> When I get mad my face gets red because I am going to cry.
> I tighten my eyes which are not bright and gay but dark and
> sharp. All my hair gets in my face.

Andrea rewrote her piece. She rewrote it not for active verbs and
present tense but for the sound of her feelings.

> I'm mad. My face is red because I'm going to cry. My eyes are
> dark and sharp. My hair is in my face.
> I dig my fingernails into my hands. They get swollen but I
> don't care.
> I go stomping off. Alone, I sit down. Tears burst from me.
> They burn my face as they roll down.
> This happens mostly on the playground. When I go in, people
> whisper behind my back. Notes are put in my cubbie. "You're
> stupid." "We hate you."
> I wish I could hurt them. I try to forget it by doing my work.
> A knot is getting bigger and bigger.
>
> Andrea Squibb
> Age 8

When Rebecca listened to her piece, she changed not only the
words but the form of her writing. "I can hear a poem in this,"
she said to me. I listened while she read the draft to me.

> I crunched over to some snow on the driveway. I walked on
> top of the icy snow to a big boulder. The plow had pushed it up.
> I sat, my legs dangling. Then I rose, proudly onto my glittering
> throne. I felt like a king. I grabbed an ice-covered stick, my staff.
> I sat on the snowy boulder, my throne.
> "Rebecca, come help shovel." I slide off the shiney snow and
> turn into me again.

I watched Rebecca work to make this into a poem. Over and
over, she whispered the lines, "I grabbed an ice-covered stick, my
staff. I climbed onto the snowy boulder, my throne." She heard
the rhythm of her words as a dancer feels the rhythm of a song.
Responding with it, she took her pencil and added more words,

more lines. Again she read the lines outloud. Listening, listening.
This is her poem.

> I rose onto a snowy boulder,
>> My throne.
> I grabbed an ice-covered stick,
>> My staff.
> Icy snow sprinkled on my face,
>> My veil.
>
> "Rebecca! Come help shovel."
>
> I clambered off the snow,
>> Me again.
>
>> Rebecca Lavine
>> Age 9

In her poem, Rebecca never *tells* her reader it was a snowy day
and she was pretending to be king. She shows this. She has learned
to imply, to suggest, to show rather than to tell. She deliberately
puts in and leaves out, plays up and plays down. She has learned
to pack meaning in between her lines.

This is not unique to poetry. When my children read what they
they have written, they search for words which can be omitted, for
meanings which can be inferred. Becky's first draft read like this:

> A flying yellow speck was near me. "A bug," I thought. I
> shooed it away. Then, "Ouch!" That bug was a yellow jacket
> and it had just stung me.

She rewrote it to read·

> A flying yellow speck buzzed around my finger. I shooed it
> away. Ouch! The sting felt like a knife, cutting into my finger.
>
>> 'Becca Paoletti
>> Age 8

When children learn to write with inference, they learn to read
for suggested meaning. What is the writer trying to say? Why has
he chosen the word *frail* rather than *fragile*? What has happened
before this incident?

Children who write and read, rewrite and reread, experience
first-hand the choices every writer faces. They discover that
writers deliberately choose their subjects, the perspective, and the
design of their writing. Where can a writer grab hold of the subject? What path will lead readers to the main point? What point of
view and what time sequence should be used? These are the questions an author asks, and they are the questions the child who
writes can learn to ask.

Add Your Own Writing to the Load

Janet Kovach
Edison High School, New Jersey

There is a sane, productive way to "handle the paper load" in my large creative writing class: add my own writing samples to the pile. Only in this way can I generate and maintain enthusiasm for the thousands of words on the hundreds of blue lines. Writing the same assignments that students write is my personal key for reacting to, and commenting on, their papers.

Active participation forces me to experience first-hand the dark corners of the assignments I so easily dictate. Where can I find my characters? What if I've never been in a hurricane before? Why can't words show how beautiful Bermuda waters are? Why is it so hard to write like an eight year old thinks?

Writing blocks like these are tough and frustrating, yet they must be overcome. Meeting them in my own writing enables me to understand the problems of my students at a deeper level and to offer more constructive help. My authority figure fades as they see me struggling with the same problems they are facing.

The room is very quiet during these writing times; we respect each other's need for long stretches of uninterrupted thought. A large supply of paper is on the desk, and the only sound heard is the brushing of corduroy or denim as someone walks to the paper pile to grab four more sheets. Time is forgotten as each of us becomes totally involved in shaping fragments of thought into written sentences. Writing is a draining and exhausting experience, but a very satisfying one. The class-changing bell is resented because we have more to say.

The day after the rough draft of an assignment is completed, we have a general discussion of rewrite goals. We view our own writing "coldly," much as an editor would if the piece were submitted for publication. What do we like about the writing? Where have we fallen short of our best? Does the writing really communicate what we intend it to? Are colors, sounds, textures, and smells given enough emphasis so that the reader can "experience" our writing? Will the reader want to finish the story?

Problems are shared, clarified, and often solved. If another writer faced a writing block and worked through it successfully, that writer's experience spurs the rest of us on.

Following this "writing group therapy" we complete individual goal sheets, spelling out exactly what we intend to improve. Rather than being discouraged or bogged down, we are anxious to move forward.

The next session finds us writing our second copy—not "final," but "second." I encourage students to think of their writing as in transition, not finished. Each week I clip and post interviews with authors from book club advertising and literary sections of newspapers. Learning that successful writers often rewrite many times reassures students that rewriting is a natural part of growth.

Students are free to exchange work with each other at this stage and often do. They enthusiastically discuss origins of ideas, possible twists of plot, and alternate endings. They are quite honest and open in their opinions of each other's work, and they usually give and take criticism graciously.

Second copies are then routed through me for my reactions. My particular teaching situation in a New Jersey public high school requires me to grade their creativity so I tag the last page with either an "Excellent" or a "Good," depending on the individual's effort to improve. Students are not pitted against one another for marks. I also comment about how I felt as a reader (not a teacher) of the writing. Praise builds up a young writer's ego; criticism provokes him or her to find out why I had that particular reaction. Open discussion does not always lead to agreement, and I encourage students to think of me as only one reader with one set of reactions; my word is not gospel.

This year I am using as a text a book recommended by NCTE, *Teaching and Writing Popular Fiction: Horror, Adventure, Mystery, and Romance in the American Classroom*. The author, Karen M. Hubert, provides excellent, short, stimulating writing springboards she calls "recipes." I use these to help students build to longer works. By the end of the semester each student has completed four short stories: one horror, one adventure, one mystery, and one romance. Best of all, despite the paper load that has come past my desk, I too have had the satisfaction of completing four original short stories.

Because I have taken the time and the opportunity to *write with them*, not *wait for them*, I have also grown as a writer. And the paper load has been handled more efficiently and more effectively.

3 Student Self-Editing

Errors Analysis: Fewer Errors and Faster Grading

David Drost
Woodridge, Illinois

Many teachers are convinced that students understand more rules of composition than they apply to their own writing. On quizzes, for example, students often identify sentence fragments and dangling modifiers, insert appropriate punctuation, and correct subject-verb disagreement; yet they continue to make these errors when they write. Indeed, students are capable of identifying errors in the writing of *other* students, but again they often fail to recognize these errors in work of their own. Finally, and perhaps of greatest frustration to teachers, students can correct errors that someone else has marked on their own papers but continue to make similar errors in subsequent compositions.

Over the past four years, a group of English teachers at South High School in Downers Grove, Illinois, have been testing an approach that they hope will help students eliminate their *own* errors consistently and in a relatively short period of time. This approach is called Errors Analysis, and its goal is to ensure that students understand their own errors. In short, the procedure requires students to explain in their own words why each error marked on their papers is in fact an error. To demonstrate that they do indeed comprehend the principle involved, students must also supply a corrected example—a similar sentence without error. If a student does not offer a specific explanation, the analysis is not accepted. For instance, "I need a comma" is not an adequate explanation of a punctuation error; "When a dependent clause comes first, follow it with a comma" is specific and acceptable. Similarly, "This is a poor topic sentence" is not an adequate explanation of a paragraph error; an acceptable explanation might be, "The main idea of this paragraph is how people talk, but the topic sentence does not mention this characteristic." A more detailed explanation of this procedure may be obtained by writing directly to the author.

In order to determine whether or not Errors Analysis really accomplished what we hoped it would do—enable students to understand and eliminate their own writing errors—we divided 360 tenth, eleventh, and twelfth grade students into control and experimental groups. The sex distribution was equal, and the ability levels included honors classes, average classes, and classes of students with low motivation. All classes were assigned the same one-paragraph, in-class composition at the beginning of the course and a similar composition at the end. Students in the experimental groups completed an Errors Analysis after each writing assignment, but students in the control groups wrote an additional paper instead. In other words, control students wrote twice as many compositions as did students assigned to experimental groups.

The Test Data we collected from the pre- and post-course paragraphs suggest that the number of writing assignments was less important in improving writing skills, particularly in reducing the number of mechanical errors, than was the student follow-up on their mistakes through Errors Analysis. This was especially true in three areas: mechanics as defined by our current text, use of supportive detail to establish the topic sentence, and paragraph unity. Although students in the control groups wrote twice as many compositions, they made more errors on the final in-class writing assignment than did the students in the experimental groups who had applied the Errors Analysis technique to their graded papers.

One of the most interesting aspects of our study is the effect that Errors Analysis might have on the time teachers spend grading student writing. The first Errors Analysis is time-consuming to grade, but the grading time decreases with each assignment. Students quickly learn that the fewer mistakes they make on the original assignment, the fewer errors they will have to analyze. By the end of the semester, many students were writing papers with no errors, and the total grading time for compositions had decreased.

It is only fair to point out that students in the Errors Analysis groups inundated teachers with a shower of questions when the procedure was initiated. The first time a teacher assigns an Errors Analysis, therefore, he or she should plan on spending one or two periods answering individual questions and helping students to identify what they do not understand. Another initial but temporary problem with Errors Analysis is that some students have been making the same error for years and resent being asked to explain something they were supposed to have learned years ago. As one student humorously remarked, "I never had to understand it before, just change it." Often these students are embarrassed. They don't want extra attention from the teacher. They would much prefer merely rewriting their work as they have done in the past without drawing attention to the fact that they don't understand their errors. Sometimes these students resent a teacher's help if there are peers nearby. A simple way to allow such students to save face is to distribute a "List of Common Errors," a list which includes page numbers in the textbook where students can find an explanation of their errors. Supplementary handouts explaining common errors are also useful. After the initial shock, students will begin helping each other, and that turn of events also reduces the deluge of questions addressed to the teacher. With each Errors Analysis, the teacher needs less class time to answer questions.

As the cloudburst subsides, a rainbow appears, for the Errors Analysis students begin spending more time planning and writing each assignment. Before one teacher began using Errors Analysis, for example, the average student finished a one paragraph in-class essay in less than twenty minutes. Now every student takes twice as long. Furthermore, many of the common oversight errors virtually disappeared in the Errors Analysis groups. When students were asked about these improvements, they replied that they now spent more time writing and checking their paragraphs because they did not want to spend so much time looking up and explaining each error. Many English teachers feel that the time spent trying to correct the repetitive errors of carelessness is one of the least rewarding aspects of teaching English. This system alleviates that problem.

Errors Analysis can result in rapid improvement for students and in reduced grading time for teachers. Errors Analysis encourages students to avoid errors of carelessness and to improve higher level writing skills, for example, maintaining paragraph unity and developing specific details. Even though considerable time must be given initially to answering questions and reading the analyses of errors, after a few assignments students make fewer errors and spend more time trying to write an error-free paper. As students accept more responsibility for the accuracy of their writings, the teacher spends less time in grading; at the same time the Errors Analyses become shorter. Before the end of the first semester, many students will be making *no errors*.

Finally, data from our study suggest that student writing improves more rapidly when students spend time analyzing the corections the teacher marked on the previous assignment rather than on writing a new assignment (and possibly making the same errors again). This finding suggests that within limits more papers and more hours of grading are not necessarily the best use of student or teacher time.

The Writing Contract

Gillian C. Bartlett
Don Mills, Ontario

The following version of a contract system is ideal for those who want students to write more frequently and at greater length, become more skilled at proofreading and reach a wider audience with their writing, and still work at an individual pace without overwhelming the teacher with papers to grade. The scheme involves a certain amount of preparation, but once it is established, it operates remarkably efficiently and requires little teacher supervision.

Stage 1: Composing the Contract

Before drawing up the contract, the teacher must determine how much class time can be devoted to writing. The contract, as presented here, requires a minumum of two forty-minute periods per week at the junior high level for a term of ten weeks. The teacher must also determine what constitutes a reasonable number of errors that can be tolerated in any paper submitted. This number will, of course, need to be adjusted according to the grade level and writing abilities of the students concerned.

The contract requires students to produce ten "successfully completed" compositions in order to earn 100 percent. While this requirement as well as the definition of a "successfully completed" paper is flexible, steps 1 through 6 as listed in Part A must be included in any contract. The proofreading record sheet referred to in steps 2 and 3 also can be modified as needed.

Stage 2: Assignments and Records

Each of the assignments for the contract, specifying topic, procedures for getting started, paper length, and other guidelines, should be available as handouts for students who wish to surge ahead of their fellow students. They will also need a supply of proofreading record sheets similar to the model given here but adapted to suit grade level and abilities.

It is wise to have a highly visible record of the students' progress. This could take the form of a chart posted on the bulletin board listing the students' names and ruled with numbered columns for the assignments. As each paper is completed, the student should mark the chart in some acceptable fashion. In addition, the students should keep their compositions in folders stored in the classroom so that students, teachers, and even parents can review earlier work.

Stage 3: Writing Classes

Approximately once a week the teacher formally introduces a new assignment to the class. Although students will be working at vastly different rates, this schedule will help them pace themselves by providing motivation.

During class periods, the students should be involved in one of the following activities:

a. discussing ideas for an assignment with a classmate;

b. composing a rough draft;

c. proofreading a classmate's paper (no one student should be asked to proofread more than two compositions in a single period);

d. discussing with a classmate his or her rough draft;

e. writing the final copy of a composition;

f. recording a successfully completed composition and placing it in his or her file folder.

The teacher will, of course, either be reading final copies or helping students with particularly difficult writing problems.

Stage 4: Evaluation

Under this contract system the teacher is free to enjoy and respond to the content of the students' compositions without worrying about catching errors and assigning specific grades. If there are more than the allowable number of errors, the teacher

Writing Contract

Part A: Requirements

Your composition mark this term will be based on the number of *successfully completed* compositions which you submit to me during the term. For the purpose of this contract, a successfully completed composition is one which contains *no more than* ONE major sentence error, and no more than three other errors (spelling, punctuation, paragraphing, etc.). In addition, each composition must fulfill the individual assignment requirements of length, topic, and form. Assignments will be distributed as you require them.

Before the composition is submitted to me for credit, you should:

1. write a rough draft which you check yourself for errors;
2. have the composition proofread by two other people (at least one of whom must be a student in this English class) using the proofreading record sheet;
3. rewrite the composition and staple it to the rough copy and proofreading record sheet.

When I have checked your composition and marked it as being *successfully completed,* you should:

4. put the completed composition in your folder;
5. indicate on the writing chart that you have completed this assignment;
6. begin the next assignment.

Part B: Marks

If you fulfill *all* of the above requirements, you will receive 10 percent of the composition mark for each assignment successfully completed, up to a maximum of ten assignments or 100 percent.

Part C: Agreement

I am aware of the requirements for obtaining credit for a *successfully completed* composition and that my composition mark will be based upon the number of these successfully completed compositions which I submit.

Although I am entitled to change my mind, at this time I would like to receive a mark of _____ percent for this part of the English course for Term III.

Signature: _____ Date: _____

need simply underline them, return the paper to the student, and request that it be rewritten until it is satisfactory. Because the compositions have already been carefully edited and rewritten, however, the teacher is rarely faced with an error-ridden paper. Consequently, the assessment can proceed much more quickly than usual.

In addition, because students submit compositions at different times, the teacher is never overwhelmed by sets of papers which must be graded *en masse*. A natural rhythm develops with the teacher reading four or five papers a night. What is more, when the reading is done during class time, students receive immediate feedback, feedback which often involves the teacher in a discussion with the student proofreader concerning the merits of a particular assignment.

There is no question but that under this system the teacher reads far more student writing than is normal. However, because the burden of assigning grades is removed, because the teacher can actually relax and enjoy the papers, and because the work is spread evenly over the term, the "marking" seems far less onerous.

The students profit as well because their writing reaches a wider audience, including peers, older students, and perhaps parents as well. With this audience in mind, students become increasingly careful of what and how they write. On the other hand, students can relax as they write because they know that for once, only simple hard work, not necessarily intelligence or imagination, stands between them and that 100 percent.

Proofreading Record Sheet

Author: _____ Assignment No. _____

1st Proofreader: _____

2nd Proofreader: _____

Indicate in the appropriate column the number of errors found.

Error	1st Proofreader	2nd Proofreader
Major:		
non-sentence	_____	_____
fused sentence	_____	_____
comma splice	_____	_____
run-on	_____	_____
Minor:		
spelling	_____	_____
punctuation	_____	_____
paragraphing	_____	_____
tense agreement	_____	_____
other	_____	_____

Does the composition fulfill the requirements of the assignment?

1st Proofreader: _____ Yes _____ No (specify) _____

2nd Proofreader: _____ Yes _____ No (specify) _____ _____

Eureka! Moments and
Reflection Questions

Linda Shadiow
Montana State University

Making pertinent comments which reinforce high school students'
abilities to judge their own work is often the result of student-
teacher writing conferences, but with too many students, too
many papers, and too little time, I found I could hold such conferences only infrequently. I retreated to extensive red penciling
of all errors on all papers with the hope that a stray "awk" would
help at least one student experience that "Eureka" moment that
can come with pertinent help. This was far from a solution. I
searched for ways to read students' minds so my comments would
be aimed at those parts of their papers they had worked hardest
on or suffered most with. Eureka! Why not ask them?

The next time they turned papers in, I asked them to respond to
four questions:

1. What is the best part of your paper? Why?

2. What part of your paper would you spend more time on if
   you had it? Why?

3. What one word, phrase, or idea deserves the "Right On
   Award" for exceptional choice?

4. What comment would you put on this paper if you were
   teacher?

When one weary student looked up and asked, "Hey, Man, isn't
this your job?" I knew that reflection questions were overdue. We
had all been operating under the assumption that the keys to
effective writing were held only by English teachers; I knew it was
past the time for me to help them teach themselves.

That evening, instead of reading, commenting on, and correcting the papers, I read through each paper, reserving comment
until I had read that student's response to the reflection questions.
Then, rather than stabbing at all the errors under the assumption

that they were of equal importance to all students, I aimed directly at the students' main concerns. A student who felt she had finally done a good job of paragraphing commented on it in response to the first question, and I responded with a comment that supported her judgment. I know that ordinary things done with ordinary skill were often overlooked in her previous papers because of my struggle to correct everything.

The second question is designed to discover what part of the paper the student considers to be weak, but it is worded to solicit a positive rather than a negative response. One student stated that she felt her conclusion rambled and that she would have used the extra time to search for a better ending. I was able to applaud her insight and to offer some suggestions for a stronger ending. I winced, remembering I had written a red "weak" next to the wordy conclusions of some of her previous papers and that I had not given her credit for recognizing this problem herself.

Question three asks students to search for the gem hidden in every paper, so that regardless of the grade on the overall assignment, there is recognition of the fact that merit can be found in the parts of writing as well as the whole.

The fourth question gives students a chance to make an overall comment on the writing in the form of a hypothetical teacher response. The responses I have gotten have ranged from the serious, "Not as good as your last paper," through the light-hearted, "This is the best paper I have read in my 100 years of teaching," to the poignant, "Good paper even though I know your grandfather died last night."

After I had responded to the answers to the reflection questions, I returned to the papers and added the hieroglyphics my English-teacher soul seems committed to. When students got their papers back, they turned immediately to the reflection question sheet. They were pleased to be getting personalized information directed to their own perceptions of their papers. Because I continued to use the same four questions with subsequent assignments, students developed a "teacher sense" about their papers. Some students ambitiously revised drafts until their answers to the second question read, "I picked out what I needed to spend more time on before this paper was due, and I did it."

The regular use of reflection questions following written assignments helped both my students and me to experience "Eureka" moments with more regularity than was possible under our "You-hand-it-in, I'll-turn-it-back" procedures and the infrequent writing conference sessions.

Editorial Groups

Audrey J. Roth
Miami-Dade Community College

The term I began to teach composition classes with forty community college students assigned to each section was the term I decided that I had to find a way to reduce the number of papers I read while still providing enough writing experiences and support to help students. My previous attempts at various kinds of group work in the classroom had not been satisfactory. But then some reading,* some guide sheets I'd used occasionally for writing classes, and a notion that came from my own experience in writing for publication led me to try editorial groups in the classroom. They *have* cut down my paper grading, and students feel they learn more about writing from the editorial groups than from other classroom methods.

An editorial group allows each student to concentrate for several papers during the term on just one facet of composition before attempting to do everything—writing, editing, proofing— alone, which is the way we usually ask students to write. The class profits by gaining the opportunity to discuss a number of papers written by its members, and I have drastically reduced the time I spend at home reading papers. Besides increasing the students' understanding of the writing process, the editorial groups make more general use of my own knowledge of composition than the long notes I formerly wrote on individual papers.

An editorial group consists of three students, each of whom takes an assigned role—author, editor, or proofreader—in writing three papers. Each time, the group submits just one paper—a combined effort—and each member receives the grade assigned to the paper. Subsequently, each student completes one or more papers alone, fulfilling all three roles.

---

*Carol M. Jacko, "Small Group Triad: Instructional Mode for the Teaching of Writing," *CCC* (October 1978): 290-92.

The term I began using editorial groups, our text was a reader, so we discussed how its contents had evolved through the same editorial process I was asking the students to follow. I also brought in some of my own writing: drafts and revisions, evaluations by colleagues, and editorial response, galleys and page proofs. With these aids, introducing students to the concept of the editorial group was—and still is—easy.

In my classes, students form their own groups, but the grouping can obviously be handled in other ways. If, after dividing into three's, there is one person left over, she or he can work with a group; if there are two people, they form a group for which I act as proofreader for the first round. It is best for each group to remain together for the series of three papers; however, illness and attrition often make shifts necessary. So far, the natural friendliness of students and their willingness to help each other have solved the problems posed by group changes.

Group members decide among themselves who will fulfill each role for each paper. The only rule is that they must rotate the responsibilities. Students are given in-class time to work on their papers because differences in class schedules and working hours generally make it difficult for groups to get together outside of class. However, each person has the phone number of the others in the group, and students often do some of their work over the phone. When students work in groups in class, I circulate among them, answering questions, prodding, settling disagreements, and generally acting as resource person.

An editorial group begins its work by discussing writing topics. Sometimes these are based on an assigned reading or a film we have viewed in class. Sometimes they are free-choice topics. The author makes the final choice, but preliminary discussion helps an author select a topic narrow enough to elicit good writing. In effect, this is the prewriting stage we know is so important for students to become accustomed to.

Each member of the editorial group is given a guide sheet for each of the three roles she or he will eventually assume. Each guide sheet lists a number of questions to be answered by the person fulfilling a particular role, but students are encouraged to add questions or to ignore those that seem irrelevant. Experience has convinced me that students who respond to as many of these questions as possible do better in their roles than students who omit many questions—and far better than those who ignore the guide sheets entirely (which sometimes happens, at least for the first paper).

The guide sheets I use are each about a page long—too much to reproduce here, especially since teachers will want to prepare their own in accordance with the grade level they teach and their expectations of students.

The author guide sheet I distribute contains these questions, among others:

> Is the topic sufficiently narrow? Can something worthwhile be said about it in the time available for essay preparation and in a reasonable amount of writing space?
>
> Do you have enough information about the topic to begin writing about it?
>
> Do you have something you really want to communicate? Are you writing in order to fulfill an assignment or cover a piece of paper?
>
> What is your purpose in writing this piece? How do you expect to affect the audience? (The class is always the audience for this writing.) What sort of response are you looking for?
>
> Have you checked over and revised the draft copy before sharing it with your editorial group?

The author writes a draft copy of the proposed paper at home and brings it to class to share with the editor, who is the prime reviewer of the work (although the proofreader often participates in the discussion at this stage rather than simply remaining uninvolved with the paper)

I consider the editor's primary concern to be questions of structure and organization, the logic and development of ideas. Accordingly, the editor's guide sheet includes such questions as:

> What is the main idea of this piece? At what point does it become evident?
>
> What aspects of the main idea does the author develop?
>
> Does the author use examples, support, or illustration for each aspect of the main idea?
>
> Are there smooth transitions between ideas? Between paragraphs?
>
> Do you have a sense of satisfaction at the end of the essay? Of completion? Do you have any questions or doubts that need answering?

The author revises the essay on the basis of the editor's response to the first draft. Occasionally an editorial group has another conference and the editor looks at a second draft; however, the author almost always assumes responsibility for making suggested changes. I stress that only those changes the author is willing to make need be made; the editor's (and proofreader's) comments do not need to be followed if the author feels that by doing so he or she will not strengthen the composition.

Finally, the proofreader uses the proofreader's guide sheet to check over the essay. On this sheet are questions about language and mechanics, such as:

Is the language concrete? Specific?

Does the language make you, as a reader, see? hear? taste? touch? smell?

Are words used accurately?

Are there unnecessary repetitions of words? Of ideas?

Are all words spelled conventionally?

Is conventional capitalization used?

Is appropriate internal and end punctuation used?

Is there subject-verb agreement in each sentence? Noun-pronoun agreement?

Does each pronoun have a clear antecedent?

The author confers with the proofreader concerning further revisions. Finally, one person in the editorial group types the work on a ditto, and I run it off and distribute copies to each member of the class so that we can discuss the essay of each group. (I caution students that the author in each group is responsible for reading the ditto before it is turned in to me.)

A large class with many groups means that considerable time will be spent discussing the essays. Although students say they learn the most from these class discussions (the best of them keep notes on the papers and check their future work against the information that emerges from the discussions), I cannot always spend the time needed to go over more than two essays from each editorial group. Besides, after two rounds, the class has read a goodly number of essays together and the activity has lost its novelty and freshness. Therefore, when the third essay of each editorial group is distributed, each student also receives an individual response sheet to fill out and return to the appropriate editorial group. Thus, after two experiences with whole-class evaluation, each student becomes an individual critic.

The individual response sheets I initially used began with a series of open-ended questions based on the three guide sheets, but neither the students nor I had the fortitude to answer all the questions. I now use questions that can be answered with a checkmark in one of three columns: good, so-so, or weak. However, I encourage students to comment on individual aspects of each paper, just as I do. My response sheets are likely to contain more comments than those of the students; I also add a grade for the essay. (I also assign letter grades for the other papers from the editorial groups.) My copy of each ditto is likely to have on it comments not mentioned in class, and I try to see at least one member of an editorial group to explain those notes when the paper is returned after the class discussion.

So far, I have found few students unwilling to be part of an editorial group, to accept the group grade, and to have his or her name appear on the ditto of an essay. Those who do object are usually allowed to do individual work. I do, however, weigh the course work so that the editorial group grades are not of overriding importance in determining the final grade; students seem to prefer to be individually responsible for their own grades.

Students have responded well to working in three-person editorial groups. There are difficulties, of course. Chief among them is that some people want their ideas incorporated into a paper, no matter what their assigned role for that particular paper—and their colleagues in the group try to be helpful by agreeing. Poorer papers, therefore, seem to come from groups that fail to make distinctions about the responsibility of individuals for particular roles within the group. A second difficulty seems to involve students who fail to pay attention to the guide sheets—students who set out to prove that they know enough to get along without using this aid.

The most gratifying response I have had to this method of teaching writing comes from students in editorial groups that really tried to use the approach. They say that they worked hard to stick to assigned roles in the group, but that by doing so they gained insight into the group process as well as into writing—and they were pleased by the rather high quality papers they presented to their colleagues. Class evaluations show that the editorial group work and the ensuing class discussions of the papers are the activities students almost invariably cite as being most valuable to them in the course.

4 Practice with Parts

Divide and Conquer

Greg Larkin
Brigham Young University, Hawaii Campus

For years the cry of the desperate English teacher has been "I can't provide the kind of composition instruction I'd like because I have too many papers to read." The mathematics of the argument are simple and chilling. A high school English teacher may have as many as five composition sections of thirty students each. If these 150 students hand in one two-page essay a week, the teacher is confronted with the task of evaluating 300 pages. If a teacher can read and comment on ten essays an hour, which is a mere six minutes apiece, the job takes fifteen hours. Of course, these hours are in addition to class instruction and preparation time; in other words, they are precious evening and weekend hours. If the teacher spends two hours a night Monday through Friday, he or she still faces a five-hour weekend session to get the job done.

The situation is a little better at the college level, where teachers may have only three or four sections of twenty-five students each, which could reduce the paper load as much as 50 percent. But, since college papers are usually longer than high school compositions, even this remains a difficult and time-consuming labor.

How can a composition teacher read all these papers, comment helpfully on them, and still do all the things that most teachers and human beings have to do? The answer is, the teacher must divide and conquer. We have long realized that writing is a process that does have parts that can be studied in isolation. Granted, such divisions are arbitrary; nonetheless, they can and must be made for the simple reason that teaching writing effectively to the majority of students is, unfortunately, not the natural process of "just writing" that the gifted or experienced student follows. Modern composition texts, therefore, are organized into discrete units, such as rhetorical modes, prewriting and rewriting, or intended effects such as persuading, informing, or evaluating. To reduce the paper load, the teacher of composition must focus on certain areas in the total writing process and must find ways to involve other professionals in the rest of the writing process.

To begin this division of responsibility, the task of the teacher and grader of compositions can and should be divided into at least the following two parts:

1. rhetorical skills: prewriting, thesis generation, organization, selection of details, etc.;
2. editorial skills: sentence structure, grammar, spelling, punctuation, etc.

Students and teachers alike need to realize that an effective composition is a combination of these two skill areas.

For most overburdened teachers, the problem is caused by a combination of too many papers to read and too great a diversity of editing problems. While trying to teach rhetorical skills, which themselves would easily fill the entire course schedule, the teacher must also face a barrage of editing problems. For the teacher, the focus both in class and during the grading of papers should be on the rhetorical or compositional skills. But who will teach the editing skills? Divide and conquer.

Every high school and college should have a language skills laboratory, equipped and staffed to teach editing skills and to correct editing problems. Every student in an English class should be required to attend the lab weekly to work on the editing problems associated with assignments in English classes. As students enter such a lab, they basically follow a three-part scheme. First, they supply a writing sample, usually the rough draft of a paper written for their English class, which is read for mechanical and editing problems only. A major feature of this procedure is a standarized "prescription" sheet which lists mechanical or editing errors, along with a space to indicate the frequency of each error. The staff member checks off the errors as they are found in the student's writing sample, noting both type and number of errors. The staff member also circles (but does not correct) each error on the student's paper. In the second step, the student goes to exercise files, which are divided into sections that correspond to the prescription form. Each exercise sheet gives an explanation of the particular situation in question, followed by many sample problems for the student to work. The student studies the exercise sheet and does the problems until he or she feels confident enough to identify and correct similar errors in the original writing sample. Finally, when the student feels confident that he or she has corrected every error circled on the original writing sample, he or she returns the corrected essay to the staff member, along with the completed exercise sheets. Where applicable, the staff member may ask the student to generate new error-free sentences using the grammatical forms with which the student had trouble.

How does all this reduce the English teacher's load? The key is that the original writing sample the student brought to the lab was not just any old paper, but the first draft of the weekly essay being written for the English class. In high school, where classes usually meet daily, the weekly schedule might look like this:

Monday: Introduction to the basic rhetorical skill to be developed in the next essay. Assignment: rough draft due tomorrow.

Tuesday: The student brings the rough draft to the language lab and goes through the process described above. The English teacher uses the time to prepare for Wednesday's class or to grade papers from other classes.

Wednesday: The student brings the corrected rough draft to class, and the English teacher focuses on the rhetorical skills being developed in the essay. Assignment: write the second draft of the essay for Thursday.

Thursday: The student brings the second draft of the essay to the lab and corrects it as on Tuesday. The teacher prepares for Monday's introduction of a new rhetorical skill.

Friday: Students are assigned to pairs and evaluate each other's essays in relation to the rhetorical skills the English teacher introduced that week. Each pair's comments are noted on the student's paper along with any remaining editing problems.

Weekend: The teacher has at least begun to prepare for Monday's class, so he or she has as a main task for the weekend the reading of the same number of papers as always, but these papers have now been edited twice in the language lab and once in class on Friday. The teacher's reading job is clearly easier than before, and yet the individual student has learned more and received far more feedback than he or she did under the old system, where one teacher was responsible for teaching and correcting both rhetorical and mechanical skills.

For slower classes, or if more instruction time in the rhetorical skills is needed, this basic pattern can be expanded to fit a two-week schedule by allowing two or three days of extra instruction in rhetoric and a few more days in the lab.

An advantage of this system for the student is that the editing instruction in particular is highly individualized. Lab procedures permit concentration on individual problems that is unattainable in a "grammar" class where thirty students are forced to study one problem at a time, whether it is their problem or not. While increasing the effectiveness of editing instruction, the system also generates two extra hours a week for the teacher to prepare better lessons or to catch up on grading from other classes. The teacher does not have to spend class time answering one student's editing question while twenty-nine other students lose touch with the class.

Permutations of the system are also possible. A teacher, for example, can exchange the final essay assignments turned in Friday for those of another English teacher. Each teacher spends the weekend reading another teacher's papers. This tactic weans students away from an overdependence on their teacher's individual methods without adding to the number of essays each teacher reads. Another interesting variation (which also reduces somewhat the number of laboratory staff members) is to have composition teachers serve as lab staff members to students other than their own. This assignment eliminates the teacher's preparation time but saves money and keeps composition teachers in close touch with editing problems.

Obviously, cost is associated with a laboratory program, but it is far less than might be expected and, for the benefits received, is a great investment. Two staff members trained to read essays quickly for editing problems only can handle thirty students during an hour, especially because most of the lab work is self-instructional. Exercises for most editing problems are readily available commercially, or faculty members can generate their own and run them off on a duplicating machine very cheaply.

The key to solving the English teacher's paper load is thus to divide the teacher's and student's time and effort into two very different aspects of the composition process—rhetoric and editing. Both student and teacher focus on one skill at a time and do not confuse the two. No longer does either student or teacher confuse good writing with accurate editing. Composition teachers are free to concentrate on composing, and editing specialists can identify and solve editing problems. Ultimately, the student is the winner, for he or she is afforded the best instruction in each separate skill and then held accountable for the union of the two in the final product—a rhetorically effective and carefully edited essay.

Reducing Three Papers to Ten: A Method for Literature Courses

James C. Work
Colorado State University

It would be an exceptional English teacher indeed who has never tried to find some way to teach literature or composition without requiring extensive written work from students. We know that they need to write, and we know that the writing needs evaluation, but when midnight is approaching and there are twenty papers left to grade we cannot help wishing there were another way. Even in my sophomore survey of English literature, where I required only two or three papers in a semester, I had to look forward to those days when I would live with a stack of thirty-five or more essays until they were done. Four years ago, while planning how to work those essays into a semester syllabus for my college students, I finally arrived at a way to avoid them.

My answer to the problem of grading three sets of papers was simple. Instead of three themes, I assigned ten.

The problem, as I saw it, was twofold. In the first place, my usual class load of two composition courses and two literature courses simply would not allow me to do justice to the writing of all students. The writing done for the literature courses was being sacrificed in order to leave time for the composition courses. Quality was the second problem. The papers written in the lower-division literature courses tended to be too general or too complex. Some topics took the students into research projects which had already been thoroughly covered by published scholars. Some were hardly related to the literature being read; many ended up being padded out with meaningless details or vapid generalizations.

I determined that I needed a new method for assigning papers in lower-division literature courses, and I knew that it had to meet at least four criteria.

1. Students of literature should write about literature—tests are not in themselves adequate either for learning or for the evaluation of students' ability to read and think.

2. Student writing should be graded and returned within a week—preferably in the class period following the submission.

3. Written assignments should concentrate on the literature being studied and on such scholarly commentary as is appropriate to the purpose and academic level of the course.

4. Assignments should be such that they can be graded quickly, fairly, and according to a clearly understood set of standards.

Everything about the situation pointed to one solution: assign short essays which could be written according to strict rules and graded by fair standards. I discussed the situation with the sophomore survey class I had that semester, and got them to agree to be my experiment group. The text was *The Norton Anthology of English Literature*. Course requirements included regular attendance (taken by a pass-around attendance record), two "objective" examinations (in the fifth and tenth weeks), a two-hour essay final examination, and ten experimental essays. We dubbed these our "microthemes."

The following information sheet and sample were distributed. Two more samples of microthemes accompanied the instructions. I later distributed copies of the four best microthemes from the first set and spent the better part of an hour discussing their strengths.

I was surprised to find how quickly I could grade each set of microthemes. After the first few sets, which had to be done with extra care and with directional comments, I could get through a set of thirty-five cards in just over two hours. Another unanticipated advantage was size. I could carry a set of cards around with me and grade one or two in those odd moments I encountered off and on during the day.

The microtheme is also enjoyable to teach. A student can come into the office with a general idea for one, or with no ideas at all, and leave with a fairly complete rough draft. Students quickly learn the advantages of being concise, exact, and correct; after all, they have no room to be anything else. In introductory literature courses, I have used the microtheme to teach the thesis sentence, unity and coherence, paragraph development, precision, revising for condensation, and, of course, some literary analysis.

Frequency—or perhaps I should say scope—is a primary advantage of the microtheme. I set the due dates on the course syllabus in such a way as to allow a choice of authors for each microtheme.

Microtheme Instructions

On a 5 x 8" note card, describe how a passage in a Norton introduction re-lates to one of the literary pieces assigned. These "introductions" include sections which introduce major sections of the book, individual authors, or individual pieces. Some footnotes are also applicable.

Be exact—use page numbers, quotations, titles. Underline all titles used. If you revise a graded microtheme, hand in the original with it.

Grading is by word, and due to the limited space, very few critical com-ments will be used. If you want to have a graded microtheme criticized in detail, either give it back to me with a note to that effect, or bring it to the office. The words used as grades are as follows:

"Impressive" = A. Your point is clear, exact, intelligent, and supported.

"Good" = B. You read the passage accurately and applied it to the liter-ature well.

"O.K." = C. Adequate. You see the editor's point and apparently under-stand the example. You may have failed to see the important connec-tion.

"N.G." No Grade. Your point is too obvious, or your discussion too abstract, or you have misunderstood either the editors or the author of the literary selection.

In the sample below, notice the card size, the endorsement form, the title, etc.

Poetic Freedom and Learning—Dryden	Student Name
Date	Microtheme #——

On p. 1759, the editors state that Dryden "helped to order taste and critical standards, while he sacrificed nothing of that freedom without which the English literary genius could not function." However, in keeping with the general 18th century attitude toward learning (p. 1686), Dryden does seem to deny literary genius the freedom to be "unlearned."

Dryden's reluctance to permit literary geniuses to be unedu-cated is particularly evident in his discussions of writing, criticism, and the classics. He urges aspiring poets to study Aristotle and Horace (p. 1766); he compares Chaucer to Homer and Virgil (p. 1768), Shakespeare to Homer (p. 1764), and Jonson to Virgil (p. 1764).

In addition, Dryden's advice to writers—in *Essay of Dramatic Poesy*—is so full of Latin quotations that a writer seeking to fol-low Dryden's suggestions would get very little out of them, unless he had mastered the language of early Rome. The poet, unless he is a truly great genius *and* "lucky" as Shakespeare was (p. 1763), may only enjoy the "freedom without which the English literary genius could not function" *after* he has his Latin learned.

This semester, for instance, the microtheme schedule looks like this:

Microtheme	1:	Dryden or Congreve
"	2:	Addison, Steele, or Swift
"	3:	Pope or Johnson
Exam		
Microtheme	4:	Burns or Blake
"	5:	Wordsworth
"	6:	Coleridge or Byron
"	7:	Shelley or Keats
Exam		
Microtheme	8:	Tennyson
"	9:	Browning
"	10:	Arnold
Final Exam		

(Mill, Newman, or Huxley may be substituted for *one* of these.)

With such a schedule, the student has the advantage of writing—and reading—about ten authors rather than just one or two. The disadvantage, if it is one, is that students do not have the opportunity to pursue broad topics or to do library research; however, it is my opinion that these are not really essential functions of survey or introductory courses.

I am well pleased with the results of the microtheme experiment. I have no more long papers to labor through, my grading time has been greatly reduced, and I have more opportunities to help individual students with their writing. I have not detected any notable change in the grade patterns, either. Each class seems to have a few A students who will hand in a B or two during the semester, and each class has a few who get D or F for not turning in all the required microthemes, or who get NG grades and do not bother to revise them or come in for help. The objective examinations also help keep the grading fair.

For the last two years I have asked students to take home and fill out, anonymously, a questionnaire about microthemes. The questions and summaries of the replies follow.

What is the average length of your microthemes? Three hundred words. Answers ranged from 200 to 500.

How do microthemes help you to understand the literature selections? A typical answer: "They require me to look in the selections for specific themes, ideas, notions, techniques, mechanics, etc. to prove or disprove information in the introductions. They make for much *closer* reading." The vast majority of replies—over 80 percent—mention rereading. All replies to date have been positive, saying that the microthemes *do* help.

How do they help you in understanding the editorial material? A typical answer is: "Because I know I might use the editorial material in an upcoming microtheme, I really have to concentrate on it, so that when I go on to the works which follow, I can pick up ideas for the themes. Again (as in the question above), I often reread editorial sections and footnotes to facilitate subsequent microtheme writing." The great majority of replies are positive. One student said the editorial material was not that hard to understand, and several (one or two per class) have said they would rather write "on what we think instead of what the editors say."

What's the difference, to you, between writing two long papers (of about ten pages) and writing ten microthemes? Which do you prefer, and why? Typical answers report that there is greater opportunity for variety, that more information is learned, that short regular essays are easier to fit into a busy schedule, that they reinforce the reading assignments, that they reduce the tendency to "skip" reading assignments, that there is less pressure involved, less time involved, and more of a chance to "redeem" a low grade. Students also say that microthemes have made them more critical readers. The words "more interesting" and "more enjoyable" appear frequently in the evaluations. Fewer than 10 percent have said they would prefer long papers.

Would you prefer extra testing instead of microthemes? "No." (No affirmative replies to this question so far.)

Is the purpose of the microthemes clear to you? "Yes." (About half the replies go on to repeat the purpose.)

Is the marking and grading procedure adequate? "Yes." (The few negative replies here have said "yes—it might be a little tough" and "good procedure. Though 'impressive' is hard to get!")

What difficulties do you have with microthemes? About half the replies say "none." The rest say there are too many of them, or that it is difficult to find topics, or that it is hard to be specific, or that it is hard not to be "obvious."

Finally, I would like to know whether you feel that doing microthemes has helped your writing ability in any way. Because of the importance of this question, I shall quote some typical replies in full (with emphasis on "typical").

"I appreciate the informality—no footnotes, etc. The themes, because they relate editorial material to the actual selections, demand more logical reasoning."

"Yes. It has made me write much more succinctly. It is much better to have to condense material while making it more meaningful than to have to have X number of pages or X number of words in a paper. The latter leads to—what else?—wordiness."

"They provide constant practice in composition. . . . It might be more accurate to say that the microthemes help my thinking ability more than my writing ability."

"Yes—I have had the worst habit in papers of being too wordy, too unorganized, and of repeating myself—in the microtheme I have to state my business clearly, concisely in a shorter space—I can't use space 'fillers.'"

"How? It has helped me be more concise—helped me *look* deeper into material for significant themes instead of skimming the top. It has helped me formulate my ideas carefully—I am more particular about the opening sentence than ever before, and word selection, and that very important concluding point."

"It helps, just in the way I get practice writing every time I write a microtheme. Which is often."

"I think so. As I've said before—in order to present critical commentary in just three paragraphs or so you must be very precise as well as concise. You have to isolate the important ideas you are going to present. You can't get away with the 'blanket approach' and just bullshit your way through."

"Yes, the microthemes help me cut out all the B.S. I would normally put in a longer paper. . . . I wish other classes used microthemes."

"Absolutely—being given to 'inflated rhetoric,' the microthemes force me to get to the point immediately, since they are only one or two sides of a card long: in order to make a point or connection it's necessary to be terse and laconic.

Two or three students have claimed that they have noticed in their own writing "little, subtle improvements which come as a direct or indirect influence from the writers studied." Otherwise, the responses are nearly unanimous in claiming improvements in organization, conciseness, and precision. The only negative reaction so far came from a student who claimed that the limited space led to tiny writing and thence to poorer penmanship.

In the hope that the microthemes can speak for themselves, I would like to offer a few samples. They come from different survey classes and different years, and they differ in quality—but I won't give the grades and thus deny the reader the pleasure of assigning his or her own grades of "Impressive," "Good," "O.K.," or "NG." In the original form, each of the following was either typed or handwritten on a single 5 x 8" note card—both sides, in some instances.

The Image of an Age—Dryden

"That man of letters, that rare phenomenon, in whose work the image of an age can be discerned"—this is John Dryden (p. 1703). This statement by the editors tends to limit Dryden and restrict his works to a particular time period. It is my belief that John Dryden reflects much *more* in his poems than the issues of his time. For instance, in *Absalom and Achitophel* (pp. 1713-33), Dryden is able through the use of biblical analogy to bridge two very different ages together, and at the same time, reveal through this poem many universal truths which are applicable to every era.

Power, relentless ambition, the Imperial Presidency—Dryden could have been describing a recent trauma in United States history in the following lines (302-6) of his poem:

> What cannot praise effect in mighty minds
> When flattery soothes and when ambition blinds!
> Desire of power, on earth a vicious weed,
> Yet, sprung from high, is of celestial seed. (p. 1719)

John Dean, relating his Watergate experiences in the book *Blind Ambition*, echoes over and over the famous reply of Absalom in line 376, "Desire of greatness is a godlike sin." Thus, Absalom's rebellion, Popish Plot, or Watergate, Dryden describes for us the image of an age—any age, every age.

Pope on Perfection and Taste

The editors state that "Pope assumed the role of the champion of traditional civilization: of right reason, humanistic learning, sound art, good taste, and public virtue" (p. 2138). In *An Essay on Criticism* Pope takes on this "role" and defends its attributes. In the lines

> Ah, ne'er so dire a thirst of glory boast,
> Nor in the critic let the man be lost!
> Good nature and good sense must ever join;
> To err is human, to forgive divine. (p. 2153)

Pope advises the critic that small mistakes are inevitable, and human. The critic must look at the work as a whole, and have enough "good sense" and "right reason" to know that a minor flaw need not be criticized as a major defect, thus ruining the artist when in the true sense the work collectively is "sound art."

Pope tries to inform not only the critic but also the artist that the public deserves art of "good taste," thereby protecting the "public virtue." Pope also saw that if it's genuine art, the public leaves it with an awareness of "humanistic learning" that could not have been acquired without it.

Tennyson and Myth

On p. 1011, the editors maintain that for Tennyson, ". . . it is the recorded past of mankind that inspires him, the classical past in particular." What the editors fail to mention, however, is that it is not the classical past in general, but the mythology of the past that inspires Tennyson. Perhaps it is an attempt to find some type of central core to emulate during an age where values are in transition due to rapid change.

Tennyson describes in "The Kraken" (p. 1011) a mythical beast that has slept for a millenium far beneath the surface of the ocean. This beast is destined to remain undisturbed until the fire at the end of the earth forces him to rise, and thereupon die. Tennyson could possibly be alluding to the death of mythology in his technical age.

In "The Lotus-Eaters" (p. 1019), Tennyson appears to be lamenting an age that has no sense of leisure, or the beauty of nature; a people too busy toiling to take note as "the folded leaf is wooed from out the bud." Tennyson cleverly sets the poem in the midst of the Homeric myth of Ulysses, knowing that his English audience would automatically identify. But the poem is (not clearly) a criticism of the work-ethic of the Victorians. It is also possible to interpret it as a condemnation of idleness and misplaced values.

Tennyson again uses the Homeric myth in "Ulysses" (p. 1024). But this time he approaches it from a completely different framework. It is not set during Ulysses' great voyages, but after them, when he is an old man. And he wants to return, to go back to the days of his adventurous youth. Tennyson could possibly be alluding to the loss of mythology in the Victorian era—the lack of impulse and risk-taking—the loss of ideals in a stuffy, conservative, industrial age.

These examples are from the sophomore survey of English literature, but I have also used microthemes in my Introduction to Literature course and in my general humanities course. The microtheme is workable, in my opinion, in any lower-division course for which a well-annotated text is available. I have tried it, with less clearly effective results, without the aid of text editors. In this variation students made straight comparisons between works or identified common themes.

What are the drawbacks to the microtheme? The only serious ones, in my opinion, are that it does not get students into the library to learn some search techniques, and it does not afford an opportunity to learn proper documentation form. My only defense is to say that longer papers do not always teach these things, either. Long papers are *graded*—afterward—on sources and acknowledgements, but I wonder if grading is the same as teaching.

The advantages are, to me, just what I have attempted to set down above. It takes me far less time to grade each set, and the sets come in more regularly and become part of my schedule rather than an interruption of it. I get a variety of material to read, and I have more scores to go by when computing final grades. Individual help with student microthemes takes much less time than help with long papers. I can grade harder, knowing the student has more chances to make up for low scores. And students' attitudes toward the microthemes are far better than toward long papers.

I am currently working out a way for students in my upper-level courses to do a series of microthemes which will be oriented to single statements of purpose—much like the note cards for a master's thesis or senior essay. These will involve rigorous library work and documentation methods. And somewhere in the back of my head, I am at work on a way to apply the microtheme to composition courses.

5 Focused Feedback

The Overgraded Paper: Another Case of More Is Less

Muriel Harris
Purdue University

Working in a large and busy writing lab as I do, I have seen hundreds of university students react to dozens of different methods of grading. When students come in for supplementary tutorial help, they bring along papers which have been written for a variety of writing courses and which have been graded by members of a composition staff of over 150 graduate students, faculty members, and part-time lecturers. Thus I have read papers graded according to textbook correction symbols, long endnotes, marginal comments, headnotes, mimeographed grids, and interlinear corrections, as well as papers graded analytically, holistically, and minimally (i.e., the sole notation being a letter grade). I've also talked with the students to whom all this effort is addressed, and their reactions seem to verify my conclusion that the amount of useful information students derive from a graded paper, above a certain minimum level, is in inverse proportion to the amount of instructor notation on the page.

Because it is important before beginning tutorial instruction to find out if students know what they should be working on, I usually ask what I can help them with even though I have already looked at their graded papers and the referral sheets from their instructors. Some students need help in decoding correction symbols before they can answer; others focus so emphatically on comments that refer to the improved or more effective aspects of their writing that they need time to find the suggestions for correction and revision. But of all the failures of communication between teacher and student, the saddest is that which results from an overload of diverse bits of information on the graded paper. Such papers are graded so thoroughly that the evaluation must represent monumental amounts of time, effort, and good intentions on the teacher's part. The lengthy endnotes are usually perceptive, the suggestions for improvement plentiful, and the corrections of grammatical errors thorough, but many students get almost nothing of lasting value from all this effort, except a vague sense that the instructor is either thorough or trying to be helpful.

As I watch students struggle to find the central message, or in fact any message, among such notations, I am forced to conclude that the major problem with the overgraded paper is that the instructor has lost both a sense of focus and a point of view. Like student writers without a thesis or consistent perspective, the teacher who overgrades leaps from suggestion to correction to criticism, from being an editor to a coach to a reader. In noting many things, the instructor emphasizes nothing, and many students, lost in the welter of messages, retreat. And what happens next is rather odd. Normally, we point accusing fingers at the perpetrators of unclear, overly complex, or unfocused writing. In this case, however, the receiver of this well-meaning babble is the one made to feel guilty or inadequate because he or she is unable to catch the message, while the grader, basking in a sense of martyrdom, chalks up another overworked, underpaid day.

Some students, confronted by extensive commentary, give up completely, preferring never to look at the paper again. Other students, in desperation, grab for something concrete, perhaps misspelled words or inappropriate punctuation. With an almost audible sigh of relief, they find *something* on the page that can be dealt with, changed, conquered. Another effect of the overgraded paper is that when students know that every line, every word, is going to be scrutinized, they take their writing seriously—very seriously. In one sense, such caution is admirable; in another sense it is deadly. Finger exercises, trial runs, rough drafts, experimentation—these are all part of the process of learning to write. But, unlike the athlete who is allowed to practice in order to improve skills, the writer in the over-grader's class is always playing a varsity game in the glare of the spotlight.

What then does one do when faced with the problem of wanting to talk extensively to the student, of wanting to go beyond the "nice work, shows improvement" kind of evaluation, but not so far that the student files away the graded paper with its long commentary until he or she has a free evening? A thorny question indeed, but we can work toward solving the problem by using the same checklist that we suggest student writers consider as they compose their messages: find, clarify, and limit our message; consider our purpose and audience; sort out our points of view; and choose a manner or mode that effectively conveys what we want to say. As in any composing situation, these considerations inter- act, shove up against and limit each other, enrich and reinforce each other. For the sake of simplicity, I will disentangle them here and treat them as if they were separate. The easiest to sort out is the grader's personae. We can announce this ahead of time, ex- plaining that we will look at various drafts *only* to offer sugges- tions for improvement or *only* to comment on what's working effectively so far. Or we can set up different voices spatially on the page: grammatical errors circled in the text (grader as proofreader/ editor), suggestions for improvement listed at the end of the paper (grader as coach), questions relating to lack of clarity, context, etc. in the margin (grader as audience), and so on. But even here, a a single message ought to predominate.

When the grader wishes to convey the message that further in- struction is necessary, there is no need to write out all that must be said on paper; a more effective method exists. Borrowing from our writing lab's practice of scheduling small-group sessions on various topics, I've found that a workable, time-saving solution is to hold four or five ten- to fifteen-minute small-group sessions during the class hour in which the papers are returned. The topics for these short sessions are determined by what seem to be the stu- dents' major needs, and on their papers I invite them to attend one or at most two groups during the hour. The value of the small- group meeting for the student is that it overtly labels what he or she really needs to work on. The message is clear and likely to be retained for further writing. But other messages are transmitted as well. When several people come together to discuss the need for more specific detail, or maybe for transitions between sentences, or even for correct comma usage, it is easier for them to acknowl- edge that they are working on a valid concern of writers and not on some peculiar personal deficiency. In addition, if students show up repeatedly in the same group, their presence is the clearest possible signal that they need the help of the writing lab. When the teacher leaves one group to move on to another, the first group can work on practice exercises or revise their papers. Such a follow-up helps to ensure a connected sequence of diagnosis, in- struction, and practice, a sequence that is too often interrupted when the graded paper is received and discarded immediately. Stu- dents who are particularly adept at the writing skills to be covered in other small groups can serve as peer tutors.

Flexibility and a degree of individualization are obvious advan- tages of the small-group approach. Moreover, it is amazing how efficiently ten or fifteen minutes can be used, how much ground can be covered (even on a complex matter such as organization), and how the tone of the teacher's voice can defuse a message that would appear harsh in writing. But the most useful result is that the teacher has to limit the evaluation comments to one or two points that really are important. After all, we have no right to scatter a barrage of messages across the landscape of a student's paper when we're trying to teach concepts like focus and control.

How to Grade Student Writing

R. Baird Shuman
University of Illinois at Urbana-Champaign

All of us, as English teachers, have had a common experience: we have read and graded student papers with great care and devotion—only to see the students who most need help look only at the grade, crumple the paper, and throw it into the wastebasket. As disheartening as this is, it is understandable. If the grade is low and the paper is covered with marks, any psychologically healthy student survives by pretending that it doesn't matter and by showing the contempt which will support this pretense.

Even the dutiful student who does not do this probably cannot cope with fifteen or twenty errors in a single paper. At the most, a student can cope with no more than four or five errors in a paper, and by "cope with," I mean not only correct the error, but understand the principle underlying it and avoid making the same mistake again.

Student writing improves dramatically when teachers mark no more than a set number of errors in a paper (three is my preference), draw a double line to indicate that this is the point at which they stopped marking errors, and confine the rest of the reading, as well as the written comment, to content. Students should be informed that you are doing this and should understand both why you are doing it and what their next responsibility is.

In the margin, the first error should be noted with the number "1." The material in the text of the paper that contains that error may be circled or underlined. After the marginal number should appear a question such as, "Why do you need a comma here?" or "What does this word mean? See your dictionary." No student paper should be considered complete until each question has been answered and the correction made.

In addition to limiting the number of errors marked, teachers should also be sure to indicate to students what is strong about their writing. Positive statements encourage students to think about commendable elements of their style which they might develop further. In working with and keeping careful records on 544 high school students over a three-year period, I found that substantial gains appeared in the writing of most of them when I limited my detection of errors to three and when I tried to emphasize something positive in every piece of writing. The most notable change was that fewer and fewer of them repeated the same errors once they were required to explain what was wrong with a given construction and why it was wrong.

One other technique is that of telling students that they have to write every week, but that you will give thorough readings to only about one-fourth of the papers they hand in. In the others, you will focus on one random paragraph and will read only that paragraph, marking it with a check. A variation on this procedure is to have students write as many as two or three papers a week, keep them in a folder, and, periodically, perhaps once every fortnight, select from the folder the one paper on which they wish to be judged for that period.

Objectives for Our Own Composing Processes—When We Respond to Students

David A. England
West Virginia University

What do you try to accomplish when you read student papers? That is a question many teachers find hard to answer. In spite of having read countless sets of themes, experienced teachers often have only vaguely formed objectives and strategies in mind as they move from the top of the pile to the bottom. And yet, without objectives to focus our responses, our comments to students can be vague and incomplete. By working from a list of objectives when we respond to student writing, we can make sure we say enough without saying too much and that what we say reflects a consistent notion of what growth in writing is all about. Rather than merely trying to justify a grade, to "prove" to a student that I have read the paper, or to mark all the errors, I try to meet the following six objectives when I read a theme.

Objective One: Give students a reason for wanting to write again. Perhaps nothing is more important than understanding how what we say about one piece of writing influences how the student feels about his or her *next* piece of writing. We must directly help students to generate future writing tasks, whether as an expansion, as a revision, or as a "take-off" from the piece we are responding to. Comments such as the following illustrate how this objective might be met:

a. I see you approaching an interesting new idea in your last paragraph, Bill. Perhaps in a future paper you could focus more directly, maybe entirely, on your observations of the behavior of others at the rock concert.

b. Jim, if you decide to do a revision of this, see what impact including more concrete details of the accident would have on your reader. Specific description like that in your second paragraph may help your reader more fully understand the event.

    c. Karen, did you consider adding a paragraph at the end of your paper to summarize your response to the story? If you did add a paragraph, what key points would you include?

We must remember, then, that our comments do influence students' attitudes about future writing in our class. Meeting this first objective will help them discover further refinements or extensions of each assignment.

Objective Two: Help students perceive the process of composing. By regularly referring to steps in the composing process, we can help students understand the developmental process through which they work in writing a paper. Writers at any level follow a generally identifiable process in moving from initial idea to finished product. Whether we acknowledge a step in the process the student has fully considered or a step in the process that the student needs to reconsider, our comments should reflect our own perception of the writing process. For example, we might suggest:

    a. I see evidence of careful preplanning and organization in the first half of your paper, Beth. But after your third paragraph, I am not as certain about where you are going with your thesis. How is the second half of your paper related to your opening paragraphs?

    b. I can see that when you read the story, Mike, you recorded a good many details to use in your discussion of the writer's tone. However, do you feel you noted enough examples from the text to support what you say about the author's use of figurative language?

    c. I do not think you spent sufficient time in your final editing, Paul. That you left two words out of the last paragraph is evidence enough. Your overview of the play's technical aspects is quite sophisticated; don't let a lack of care in final editing turn your reader off.

We need, then, to remind our students to be concerned with the composing process, whether in planning, writing, or revising. Our comments on their papers should reflect our *own* sense of the composing process.

Objective Three: Ask students questions about the choices they have made. Meeting the first two objectives may meet the third; that is, when providing impetus for future writing and discussing the composing process, we may ask questions of the writer. Asking questions is an important strategy for several reasons. Over time, students will begin to anticipate our questions and "answer" some of them in advance. Questions help to establish a dialogue between the teacher-responder and the writer. And, obviously enough, asking a question encourages a response which can be made only after the writer reconsiders what he or she has written.

The following stems are useful in formulating questions. Did you consider . . . ? What would be the effect if . . . ? Do you think your audience will be able to . . . ? Why did you use . . . ? How many alternatives to _____ did you consider? Can you find examples in your paper where you . . . ? Diction, syntax, general organization, mechanics, and steps in the composing process can thus be called to the student's attention in such a way that he or she will become more aware of the choices made and the options available. Through our questions, students learn to substitute fully considered, conscious decisions for the relatively "unconscious" ones the unquestioning, and unquestioned, writer all too easily makes.

Objective Four: Directly point out one or two grammatical, mechanical, or syntactical problems.

Objective Five: Always make one suggestion about larger rhetorical strategies. Objectives four and five might be met concurrently with any of the first three, and I discuss them together here because each focuses on the need to suggest specific ways a piece of writing can be improved. The specific direction of these two objectives reminds me at once that my "error hunting" must be limited and that it must be limited to only those problems I am certain the writer can rectify. It is all too easy to point out too many problems, and in the process point out more than can be assimilated by the writer. Objective four focuses my attention on word and sentence-level deviations from standard written English; objective five reminds me to consider larger rhetorical problems which may be an impediment to effective exposition.

Consider the nature of such comments as, "In general, you need to be more specific" or, "You need to think more about organization" or, "Sentence structure is a problem here." With such observations, the teacher succeeds only in raising questions in the writer's mind; the questions, however, do not lead to solutions. Conversely, by limiting our comments to the most serious problems and by being specific about a rhetorical or a syntactic problem, we can answer both the "Where?" and the "What can I do about it?" questions for the student. Consider these examples:

a. In your first paragraph, you use only simple sentences. Throughout your paper, a lack of sentence variety is a major problem. Could you combine the second and third sentences in paragraph one? Find other places in succeeding paragraphs where you might combine two short sentences in order to achieve a more varied style.

b. You seem to be pursuing two separate topics in your second paragraph. Elsewhere, too, you have more than one topic sentence in a paragraph. In paragraph two, identify two specific topics; then, decide if you want to eliminate one or develop a new paragraph treating it. Ask the same question and try the same strategy in paragraphs four and five.

c. You have avoided overuse of pronouns, Bill. But sometimes when you use two proper nouns and a pronoun in the same sentence, I have trouble knowing which noun your pronoun refers to. Find two examples of the following problem in your paper: "Bill came in and Jack left because he felt sorry for him."

Objective Six: Encourage students to take more responsibility for their own learning. To many students, it seems as if *we* are totally responsible for their learning to write. Our comments should consistently reflect the more accurate notion that learning to write involves two people—the teacher *and* the student. In each response to a student theme, we should suggest one specific learning step for the student to take before writing again:

a. Robin, before writing again, demonstrate to me that you know when to use *their, they're,* and *there!*

b. Kelli, I cannot always tell which word some of your modifiers are supposed to modify—see the two underlined sentences. Before your next paper, work through the examples in handout 14 (misplaced modifiers).

c. Jamie, your last paragraph contains a nonsequitur. Read pages 433-34 in your text and then explain to me why your last argument is fallacious.

If we regularly give individual students something specific to do between writing tasks, we will be assuring them that they, too, have a responsibility to work toward their improvement. And, if we hold students accountable for what they know to do—or to avoid—when they write, we will not need to see the same errors repeated again and again by the same writers.

The inevitable response of the teacher who thinks about meeting these objectives is, "Sounds fine, but won't it take a lot of time to meet six objectives for each paper I read?" Not really. As pointed out earlier, several objectives can be combined, as the following summary comments indicate:

a. This effort could easily lead to a further exploration of dreams, Roger [Objective 1]. You might want to find research on brain wave activity during sleep. You did a particularly good job of limiting your thesis this time—a troublesome step for you earlier [Objectives 2 and 5]. Can you find two sentences that lack subject-verb agreement [Objectives 3 and 4]? See handout 11 in the files for a quick review [Objective 6]. How much thought did you give to audience here [Objectives 2 and 5]. I am uncertain as to whom you are writing.

b. This is the most you have written all year, Don! It is clear that you took much more time in gathering ideas for your paper. Your use of dialogue is an effective technique, but your use of quotation marks was inconsistent and broke some "rules" you can review on pages 113-14 of your manual. Do continue experimenting with dialogue—you have a good ear for it. But don't let your misuse of quotation marks detract from your reader's attention to what characters in your paper say. If you were to divide your last l-o-n-g sentence into three shorter ones, where would you make the division? Which way would be easier for your reader to follow?

c. What a delightful satire, Sandy. Your natural wit shows here! I bet you could find much on contemporary television to satirize. Don't forget the importance of maintaining a consistent tone in your writing; in some places (see what I underlined in blue) you sound quite informal ("really neat"). Before you write again, read Art Buchwald's column in yesterday's *Globe*. What comparisons can you make between the length of his paragraphs and the length of yours?

None of the preceding comments require more than five minutes to write—mainly because each grows out of the same set of objectives. Indeed, the time factor is one of the best arguments for reading student writing with specific objectives in mind, because economy in comment style *saves time.* Following logical objectives contributes to that economical, lucid style which can facilitate our processes of responding to our students.

In following the six objectives I have described, I am more confident that my comments are focused, specific, personalized, and reflective of what I know to be true and of what I want students to discover about learning to write. The question, What do you try to accomplish when you respond to a student's paper? is one we should be able to answer precisely—and our answers should be demonstrated in our every response to student writing.

The Best of All Possible Worlds: Where X Replaces AWK

Sheila Ann Lisman
Hutchinson High School, Kansas

In 1964 I left college a certified English teacher and began teaching in a junior high school. I gave a variety of composition assignments and spent hours laboriously grading the compositions, making a number of marks I had become familiar with during my own educational experience—*AWK*, *R-O*, *FRAG*. I even managed to reproduce those cryptic scribbles I had been unable to decipher as a student. For two or three years I marked away with a red Flair, regular point. (Somtimes red *and* green at Christmas. I was not without a sense of humor . . . and relevance. Those were the sixties after all!)

Finally, I had to acknowledge that students were "not benefiting" from my copious notations. In fact, they wadded up their returned papers, dashed from their desks, and gathered around the trash can like flies around syrup. In a fit of innovation, I required them to keep ALL their returned compositions in a folder in a file cabinet. By this time I was teaching in a high school, and I felt sure that more mature students would find meaning and motivation in my evaluative markings. The main advantage of the new system proved to be that students no longer rushed to the trash can to create congestion near my desk. They dutifully filed away their papers, but they continued to ignore the evaluations.

After those early struggles, I began working on an advanced degree, taking courses which gave me improved understanding of the writing process and knowledge of various teaching strategies I could employ. Although armed with new rationales and proper methods, I had to recognize that the sheer volume of the grading load remained a factor. So did student tenacity in ignoring evaluation. Too often, "revised" papers were merely cleaner copies of the original, with spelling the only conspicuous area of improvement.

It was at this point that I realized that the "burden" to improve had still not been placed on the students, while the "burden" of grading placed on me was, if anything, greater. I developed a simplified system of marking which I have termed the "X system." Basically the system involves making an "X" at the end of any line in which a mistake appears. The errors may be mechanical—spelling, punctuation, capitalization—or of a stylistic nature. In the latter case, I may place a bracket around several lines, indicating a problem with an entire section. These sections might include problems with semantic or syntactic relationships.

When I return the papers, I ask students to read them carefully and to correct any errors they discover. After making as many corrections as they can, they come to me individually to work on the remaining trouble spots. While I have not formally evaluated this method, it seems that all but the least capable students detect about sixty percent of their errors. Finding and correcting mistakes gives students confidence, insures that they proofread, and generally makes them more careful, competent writers.

Depending on the ability, academic sophistication, and frustration level of individual students, I may add more specific internal marks so that the search for errors is made less arduous. For example, I sometimes underline incorrect punctuation, make wavy lines under specific wording problems, and circle words spelled incorrectly, but I use these marks sparingly. Interestingly enough, I continue to find that students' reactions to X-ed lines are more emotional than their reactions to a host of lines, dashes, arrows, and scribbles extensive enough to pass for a Klee painting. They want to know what is wrong! I send them on their search, sometimes with the help of a partner or a small group. Finally, they come to me for help when mysteries still remain. And then they rewrite. This process generally takes two days. Library books may be read if a delay is involved.

You may be thinking that you would rather stay at home, feet propped on a hassock and favorite beverage in hand, peacefully grading, than face thirty students storming your desk. Amazingly enough, this doesn't happen, although there is a little confusion during the first few sessions. To help alleviate this confusion, assignments should be meaningfully designed. Workshops or summer sessions that offer sound programs in the teaching of composition can be helpful here. Also, when students know they will be discussing their writing, they tend to write better. They also realize they can get specific suggestions for improvement from classmates or from me.

Many options for assigning a letter grade are left to the instructor. Often I don't assign a grade until I receive the revised composition. Peer evaluation may also be used. While this system may not create "the best of all possible worlds," it comes close. Students find that writing can be meaningful instead of mundane, and for teachers, grading becomes bearable (even enjoyable!), not burdensome.

Not Grading Writing: How to Get Parents to Like It

Beverly A. Busching
Shenandoah College

When elementary teachers embark on a developmental, meaning-centered composition program, they face two problems—how to cope with marking papers and how to cope with not marking papers. Providing thoughtful responses to student writing is difficult, but it is largely a teacher's own problem, one to be solved by strategies such as peer feedback, group conferences, and the revision of selected first drafts. The problem of not marking, on the other hand, is not just a teacher's problem. When you decide not to mark all student writing, especially when this represents a change from established procedure, you usually attract opposition. This conflict, rather than classroom management problems, may cause the downfall of a new writing program.

Don't, however, give up what you feel is the best way to encourage student writing. You have support from the experience of other schools where student writing flourished when the grading of papers was replaced by other kinds of responses, such as real-world usefulness, audience appreciation, and discussions about effectiveness.

Let us assume that your new composition program is school-wide and that you are not in conflict with other teachers, your principal, or the central administration. Ideally, one teacher in a school would not be in the position of initiating a program in opposition to established procedures. (If you do not live in such an ideal world and venture into workshop writing on your own, you can use some of the techniques suggested below for communicating with other school personnel.)

How do you generate support from parents? How do you convince them that the flow of sometimes messy, incoherent, rambling, illiterate, misspelled, unpunctuated writing in a workshop program is the yellow brick road to writing proficiency rather than a mistaken step toward illiteracy? How do you convince them that these papers are often best left uncorrected? How do you convince them that individual papers do not need an overall evaluative grade in order for students to be motivated to do good work?

Parental support for innovative elementary school programs can be generated through an active campaign in four areas of communication: forceful demonstration of your commitments, continuing display of ongoing methods, display of results, and education of parents about the reasons for the program.

Let parents know, in no uncertain terms, that you are interested in the development of writing proficiency. Parents are deeply committed to the expectation that their children will attain competence in the basic areas of learning important in our society. If parents believe that you are not equally committed, you can accomplish very little. Once you have demonstrated your commitment, you will, in all likelihood, face doubt and opposition to your new methods, but you will have at least established a common bond and shifted the center of conflict away from the most deeply held values of parents. As you publicize the goals of your program, you will also be defining for parents the nature of "writing proficiency." You will have the opportunity to describe it in terms of useful competency in a variety of real-life settings. This definition, usually acceptable to parents, sets the stage for an understanding of workshop writing. Here are some methods to use in getting your message to parents.

Send a statement of the school's philosophy and a general characterization of the curriculum to all parents, perhaps as part of a school newsletter. The statement should be simple but not demeaningly simplistic. (Crestwood Elementary School, Madison, Wisconsin, has developed an excellent statement of the goals and methods of their writing program.)

Show your commitment in school activities. Display high-quality finished products. Some innovative display formats are given in the following sections and include announcements in PTA or school newsletters. Arrange for students to read their work over the loudspeaker and at parent meetings. Play-readings and mystery stories are especially popular for this kind of public performance. Writing contests usually generate favorable parent opinion, but unless they are handled carefully, competition may undermine your writing program's focus on personal development.

Let parents know that a lot of writing with serious intent is going on. If you save most of the student writing in folders, and the only knowledge parents have of your writing program is an occasional edited piece of public writing that is sent home, then they will, with reason, conclude that little writing is being done at school. If you cut down on handwriting practice and copying exercises and replace them with frequent unedited writing that is not sent home, parents may worry that less writing is being done. (If, of course, you suddenly start sending everything home, parents may conclude that very little *teaching* of writing is being done.)

Don't count on children to tell their parents. Daniel may have been a wildly enthusiastic author of a radio script about the class field trip, but when he gets home, Sue's dracula teeth and the lunch menu may be what he talks about. And if he does tell about the script, he may be like the child in the Cuisenaire math program who, after spending the afternoon multiplying in base four, told his parents, "We played with this neat new set of blocks at school." We want writing to be an enjoyable and natural process for children, encompassing word play and other amusements. But, incongruously, the better the program, the easier children find the writing process, and the less it sounds like learning to many parents. So, let parents know what you are doing. Here are some ways to get the message home.

> Have each child keep a list of his or her school writing, both assignments and personal choices. A dittoed form entitled "My Writing This Week" can provide a structure for this list. An eight-year-old boy had the following list:

> | | |
> |---|---|
> | a list of my favorite foods | riddle joke |
> | a dinner menu | a motorcycle going! |
> | carrot leaves | a letter to the cycle man how I |
> | describing my orange | feel about *The Mouse on the* |
> | sentences with modifiers | *Motorcycle* |
> | | how I feel today |

> Send a summary of the writing done for a week by the entire class. Such a summary does not capture individual variations in topic and function as well as do personal lists, but it does allow you to describe each type of writing in a way which may communicate its significance to parents. Where a child might list "my orange," you can list instead "detailed description of an orange."

Show off the results of your program. The public display of edited writing tells students that you value their work and demonstrates to parents that their children are, indeed, developing writing proficiency. The good writing of your students is your best public relations weapon. Here are some ways to display student writing.

> Gather writing in booklets. Compositions can be typed and mimeographed, or laminated and placed in a folder, or placed behind plastic in photo albums. Place an album of student writing, prominently labeled, in the school office where visitors can glance through it. Send a copy to your superintendent and the school board. Be sure that no young author's work is excluded because of poor handwriting—a child or an adult can type the paper. If children help to select the papers, their sense of literary judgment will be enriched.

> Occasionally put bulletin board displays of writing near the front office rather than always in or near classrooms. Parents of young children need to see the writing of older children, and vice versa.

> Hand bind or laminate stories written by individual students, and place them in a "Young Authors" section of the library.

Explain your school's approach. Don't underestimate parents. A few parents may have a real fixation on mechanical perfection, but most are normal people anxious that their children learn to write competently. It is difficult for parents to accept major changes in instruction when the school does not inform them of the changes and the reasons for them. Be prepared with a brief explanation, including the results of similar programs in other schools.

Don't be afraid to share with parents your misgivings about previous methods your school has used to teach composition. Some principals and teachers hesitate to admit that anything is wrong with their program, fearing that any sign of weakness will undermine the confidence of parents. But you can't have it both ways. If your old program was so good, why are you abandoning it for a new one?

If you believe that your program is experimental, let parents know this, too. Let them know that you have given careful thought to your choice of method, that you are closely monitoring the results, and that you will make the adjustments necessary to provide students with a quality education. Here are some other ideas.

Invite a visiting consultant to speak to parents. Follow the talk with small-group sessions. The consultant can visit from group to group to talk with parents in a personal way about their concerns.

Provide a "writing involvement" session for parents. Give them a writing task, and announce that they will share their work with each other. Watch the anxiety level zoom upward. Then ask parents to share their feelings about facing difficult writing tasks and their memories about their own school writing programs. After they have faced their own feelings of inadequacy about writing, most parents are ready to take a look at innovative methods. If there is time after this cathartic experience, switch your approach; involve parents in word games and other stimulating no-lose writing activities.

During your back-to-school night, ask parents to take part in a number of developmental writing exercises. They will then be better able to appreciate the value of these exercises and to understand why grading them is unnecessary, even destructive.

Keep a file of supportive professional articles for those parents who want a deeper background of this sort.

These suggestions have been offered with the expectation that you will choose from among them according to your school's needs and your own professional style. There is no one best way to communicate to parents. Once you get started, other ways will become apparent. The important thing is to get started so that new writing programs can grow and mature with the support of parents.

6 Alternative Audiences

Three Techniques of Student Evaluation

Leila Christenbury
William Fleming High School, Roanoke, Virginia

The laborious process of evaluation is a serious part of the writing teacher's job. Demanding, incredibly time consuming, it is a process which requires an almost religious dedication. Yet in my teaching experience, the evaluation of composition is not only difficult for teachers, but for most students, it is deadening. Although the student is active when he or she writes, once the composition is graded—however thoroughly, however lovingly—and returned, the process becomes passive: the student reads and usually acquiesces to the teacher's comments, but no further active involvement takes place.

While such passivity can be remedied by asking students to make corrections and even to rewrite whole essays, the process generates even more paperwork for the teacher and the same passivity among students, for it is the teacher who must evaluate and pass judgment a second or even a third time.

The solution to the paper load dilemma and to the problem of student passivity, I feel, is to involve students in evaluation. This article is a brief description of three techniques I have successfully used with three different high school classes. While the techniques are not sophisticated and do not eliminate teacher responsibility, they do shift some of the burden of evaluation from the teacher to the student. By providing the student with opportunities to become more active in the evaluative process, they help students become more aware of the components of good writing.

Before evaluation is attempted by students, the proper atmosphere must be established. It is vital that students feel that their work is interesting and valuable to their reader, whether that reader is teacher or student. For this reason, I make it a habit to read aloud to the class three or four essays from particular assignments. Not all of the essays are "A's," and I do not divulge the writer's name or stop to analyze specific points. I simply read the essay on the premise that it was interesting or unusual. With no exceptions in my experience, students enjoy listening to each other's work; they are usually curious to see if their work will be included, and they are flattered when it is. When I rely on this technique as a warm-up, student evaluation seems to proceed at a smoother pace. Students are used to listening to and possibly privately judging each other's work and have, hopefully, acquired some respect for each other's talents.

Not all types of student evaluations are appropriate for all types of students or assignments. For this reason, I have summarized here three different styles of student evaluation: one for a creative narrative, one for a creative description, and one for a standard essay. Further, one evaluation was done by a class of slow students, one by an above-average group, and the third by superior students. Finally, the techniques are easy to adapt to other assignments and to other students.

In Class A, a six-week elective course of short stories for a homogeneous group of twenty-seven below-average or slow students, evaluation had to be on a simple and readily accessible level. The students had a short attention span and tended to be off-task far more frequently than on.

The student assignment had been a creative one where students wrote stories patterned upon a surprise-ending thriller, "Four O'Clock," by Price Day. In the original story, the main character had a bizarre and malevolent power which materialized at four o'clock and which, in the end, turned against him instead of his enemies. Students were given specific criteria to follow in writing their own version, and fourteen completed the assignment. They were proud of their efforts and curious about what others had written, so reading and evaluating the creative stories seemed quite appropriate.

The first step was to collect the stories and to number them so that names would not be revealed. Then I drew a three-column chart on the board and asked students to reproduce it on a piece of paper: one column for *Essay Number*, one column for the evaluative category *Interesting*, and one column for the evaluative category *Easy to Understand*. (Although these two categories are admittedly broad—and possibly vague—they seemed appropriate for the creative stories and for the student evaluators.) Third, I wrote on the board an adjective description for each letter grade so that students would have a readily identifiable criterion to refer to: A—Great, B—Pretty Good, C—OK, D—Yuck, F—Awful. Using letter grades in the evaluation was deliberate because it is a system with which students are familiar and because it reinforces the notion that, this time, students share evaluative power with the teacher.

Once students settled down, had their charts ready, and understood the rating criteria, I read the fourteen stories, pausing after each one for about thirty seconds to provide evaluation time. (The only hesitation I have about asking a student to read the stories is the student's inability to decipher difficult handwriting.)

At the end of the final story, I collected all the rating papers. The class, after some discussion and two votes, decided to have their evaluations count as fifty percent of the final grade and my evaluation as the other fifty percent. I might note that the seriousness with which they took this arrangement surprised—and pleased—me.

With the help of one of my study hall students and a pocket calculator, I recorded each student's grade from each rater on a mimeo stencil and averaged the ratings into one letter grade. Each category was averaged and an average taken of the two. Thus, for each story, the stencil showed the story number, all of the student evaluation grades for each category, and the average grade of those categories. Although it may sound complicated, the recording and averaging took less than one class period.

My grading of the stories also took remarkably little time because I had read each one aloud and was familiar with the content.

Finally, I mimeographed the stencil of grades and returned each story with a copy, placing the student evaluation grade, my grade, and the average of the two on the front of the paper. In very few cases did my grade differ from the student grades, but I knew that students would want to see how others had rated them and would also be disinclined to trust my word for the student evaluation average.

The procedure generated genuine interest, and the class voted to repeat it during the six weeks. Students obviously felt that they had had some control over the evaluative process, and the process not only satisfied students but also saved me some home grading time.

Class B, a six-week elective course of nineteen above-average students studying the theme of "People's Peculiarities," read Addison's "The Coquette's Heart." This brief but difficult piece is an imaginary dissection of a fashionable eighteenth-century lady's faithless heart, and the physical properties of her heart appropriately reveal her personality. As a prewriting exercise, students picked out the salient features of the heart, linking them with character traits and frailties (or "peculiarities," as the course title indicates). To tie this eighteenth-century curiosity to something "real," I suggested that students write their own dissection, substituting a contemporary figure for the rather antiquated coquette. A teacher's heart, a parent's heart, a politician's heart, a truck driver's heart, a boyfriend's heart, and an athlete's heart were some of their suggestions, and the students then wrote their own dissections with veiled character comments.

The question of how accurate these dissections had been soon arose because some of the essays, although adequate, were certainly unrealistic, unrevealing, or patently unrelated to the subject's heart. Instead of relying upon the perceptions of one person —the teacher—student evaluation would offer a broader and possibly fairer assessment. Student evaluation might also, in this case, change a teacher's grading chore into a valuable class experience.

I numbered the completed essays, not to protect the authors but rather the subject matter: the point of the evaluation was to read each essay and have students guess the identity of the person to whom each heart belonged. To eliminate wild guesses, I used a matching format, listing on the board each character whose heart had been dissected in any essay. I, of course, knew how many of each character had been described (one politician, three teachers, and so forth); the students, however, did not know who had written about whom. They listened to the essays and, as with a quiz, matched on a piece of paper the number of an essay to the character they thought had been "dissected."

While reading, I craftily omitted the title of each essay and any words which clearly identified a politician, truck driver, or other figure. At the end of each essay I paused to let the students make their decisions; the essays were complicated, and rereadings were sometimes necessary.

Not surprisingly, no student's subject was correctly identified by 100 percent of the student evaluators, and very few did as well as 70 percent. These scores reflect, of course, the student writers' lack of clarity rather than the limitations of student listeners. Students were, however, intrigued by the fact that they occasionally misidentified a heart which their neighbors had correctly labeled.

Again, with student help, I tabulated the number of correct responses for each essay, converted that figure to a percentage, and wrote that percentage on the front of the appropriate paper. Students were surprised at how difficult it was for others to identify their subjects.

I noted in my grade book the identification percentage of each essay but did not count it as a formal grade. I did not grade the dissections myself. In this instance, completing the assignment and participating in the evaluation was a sufficient learning experience by itself. For my part, the time taken to calculate the percentages and to record them was minimal.

Class C, a year-long Advanced Placement group of nineteen superior students, was working on a description. Their essays had become routine and lifeless, and to make students more aware of the fact that they were beginning to bore themselves—and me—I initiated student evaluation.

I stapled an evaluation form to each completed essay and distributed the essays at random to students in the class. To protect the identity of the evaluator and, possibly, to enhance honesty, I assigned each student evaluator a number.

Each student evaluator had a list of five criteria which the class had previously discussed. The criteria specifically highlighted what I felt had become major problems, interest and originality of description, but they also included clarity, organization, and mechanics. For each criterion, students contributed comments as well as general letter grades. Students then averaged these five grades and assigned an overall grade to the essay. When they were satisfied with their evaluations, they returned the original essays and the evaluation forms to me.

These evaluations, although I reviewed them, made up the essay grades. The student comments were succinct, and I was pleased to note that the evaluators consistently remarked upon my current concern, the lack of interest and originality. Their comments, however, were more rigorous than their grades, for most students received A's and B's. Yet the high marks did not surprise me because these students were more grade conscious than those in the classes I previously described and would not, in a first-time experiment, want to penalize each other. Only frequent opportunities to make evaluation would, I feel, break these inhibitions. Nevertheless, the experience was valuable: I saved considerable time and students received fresh comments upon their work and were able to contribute insights into the work of others.

These three examples of student evaluation suggest what can be done in the classroom to save the writing teacher's time and to move students—of all abilities—away from their passive relationship to teacher evaluation. While I do not advocate complete reliance on student evaluation, I do feel that its benefits far outweigh its deficiencies. Evaluation by students liberates the teacher from the numbing process of constant evaluation. It places more responsibility upon the student, and it gives the student an invaluable opportunity to become an active participant in the total writing process, which necessarily includes evaluation and revision.

Whether the evaluative technique is as simple as assigning a letter grade that correlates with a single adjective, or as complicated as assessing the originality of a descriptive essay through comments and suggestions, student evaluation can work—and work well—in a variety of class situations and with a wide range of students. Instructive for the student and a conserver of teacher time, the judicious use of student evaluation is one answer to the problem of the paper load.

Critique Groups for Composition Classes

Isabel L. Hawley
Westfield State College, Westfield, Massachusetts

In order to develop into mature, self-disciplined writers, students need both informed feedback from a responsive audience and practice in critical analysis. Fortunately, it is possible to fill these two needs simultaneously through carefully designed group activities. The prerequisites are these:

1. a class whose members know and are reasonably confortable with one another;

2. a noncompetitive grading system (so that students will be honest with each other and themselves);

3. a room with either movable furniture or enough space to allow groups of three or four students to work together in small circles;

4. a completed composition assignment.

Dividing a class into small groups to work on a common critical task is a highly productive technique for classes from junior high through college. In general, critique groups should be random heterogeneous divisions. If the subject of the critique is to be a single paragraph, four or perhaps five students is a good size. If the critique is to deal with an entire three- to five-hundred-word composition, three is the best number, except for older, more experienced students, for whom four would be workable.

A critique group's task must be defined very specifically. It must require written feedback from each critic to each writer. Generally the task should be broken down into numbered steps, which are either written on the blackboard or handed out on dittoed sheets to be filled in. And the task should be right on that narrow ridge where it is challenging enough to be interesting, yet within the competence of the group. In most cases an entire class will work on the same critique assignment, but different assignments may be tailored to meet specific needs of different groups. In any case, tasks should always be designed so that the teacher is involved only as a resource. For this reason it is often useful to review the principles involved in the task before dividing the class into working groups.

The critique group procedure may seem cumbersome at first, but once the students understand what is to happen and why, it quickly becomes an efficient method. Each student brings to the group his or her own composition and pencil and paper for recording feedback. The critique assignment is written on the board or handed out, and each student works first on his or her own paper, making no marks on the composition itself and recording answers in numbered sequence on a separate piece of paper. A separate sheet for each student's comments insures that no bias is carried over from one reader to the next.

Ensuing rounds may follow either of two patterns. Each student in turn may read his or her paper aloud while the others listen carefully and make notes; or the papers may be passed around, so that each member of the group reads everyone else's paper. The nature of the task has some bearing in deciding which method to use—some things are easier to listen for than others. Also, students to whom the process is new or who don't know one another very well are less threatened by reading their papers aloud than by having others actually look at them. (Many flaws, including spelling and most punctuation errors, cannot be detected when the author reads.) It is wise, for this reason, to begin the term with critiquing assignments that focus on matters of content, organization, and emphasis, which can be effectively handled in the oral-aural mode.

Whichever method is followed, each student prepares a half-sheet of commentary for each of the other students. The writer's name appears at the top of the sheet, and the critic signs at the bottom. Each individual retains the sheets she or he has prepared until all the papers have been read or heard. The teacher serves as consultant-upon-request and timekeeper. It is important that each student's work receive an equal share of the group's attention, so the teacher should break in at appropriate intervals to announce that it is time to change papers (whether or not work on the current one has been completed).

When the last round has been completed, everyone gives out feedback sheets. Writers then check the perceptions of others against their own, looking for patterns of agreement or conflicting views. After each individual has spent a little time with his or her own work, the group should discuss conflicting views, asking for help from the teacher as necessary. If the papers are rough drafts, writers may do whatever they wish with the information on the feedback sheets. If they are final drafts, the teacher should allow a few minutes for those who want to make changes in their papers to do so before turning them in.

The feedback sheets themselves may be turned in with the final copy if the teacher wishes. If each paper is accompanied by its signed feedback sheets, the teacher gains valuable insight into the critical skills of the students and, if the papers are collected by groups, into the effectiveness of each work group. If the critiques are of a rough draft, the writer must be allowed to keep them in order to use them. On occasion, in order to check the effectiveness of the entire procedure, the teacher might ask each student to turn in rough draft, feedback sheets, and final draft together.

The cardinal rule for designing tasks for critique groups is to maintain a positive focus. Always the assignment should concentrate on merits—on things done well (or just plain done), not on omissions or failures. When class members have developed a good rapport with one another and when most members of the group are generally competent in mechanics, students should be allowed to point out one another's errors, especially on final drafts, but this sort of activity must never become the primary focus of a critique group.

Critique assignments can be useful at both rough draft and final draft stages. Any analysis of organization, rhetoric, or style that is appropriate to the level of the class is potentially a good critique group assignment. An eighth-grade class, for instance, can probably spend a good deal of time with paragraph structure: What is the topic sentence of this paragraph? What type of organization is used? How is this paragraph tied in with the preceding paragraph or with the following one? More sophisticated writers, on the other hand, will derive more benefit from criticism of a higher order, such as identifying figures of speech or listing concrete details and images and classifying them according to the senses they appeal to.

Topics can be large or small—identifying theses or looking for particular words used in special ways. The following assignment offers a combination of tasks within a narrow framework. Each student has his or her rough draft of the currently assigned multiparagraph composition. The teacher prepares the class for the exercise by reviewing the principal means of achieving unity (and perhaps listing them on the board), and then writes the assignment on the blackboard:

Third Paragraph

1. Identify the topic sentence.
2. Identify unifying devices within the paragraph.
3. List unifying devices connecting paragraph 3 with paragraph 2.
4. List unifying devices connecting paragraph 3 with paragraph 4.

Another exercise that can be applied to all or part of a composition focuses on pronouns—checking for clear antecedents and agreement between pronoun and antecedent, between pronoun and verb, and among pronouns with a common antecedent. Feedback in this case might take the form of questions raised by vague reference—Who is "she" in line 12?—and, competence permitting, suggested revisions of trouble spots. During this task the teacher should be especially alert to puzzled looks and other signs of confusion or uncertainty and ready to offer assistance where needed or to mediate a discussion that seems to be going awry. If pockets of ignorance or misinformation appear, it is important that they be dealt with promptly in order to keep the critique group exercise a positive learning experience and to prevent the less competent from being overwhelmed by bewilderment and frustration.

The following task, good for either rough or final drafts, provides practice in focused listening as well as in analysis on a broader scale. The assignment is a one- to two-page editorial for the class, school, or local newspaper. Students examine their own papers first, and then as each member of the group reads his or her own paper, the others make notes on the following points:

1. What is the point of this editorial?
2. What principal arguments does the writer use to support his or her position?
3. Is the writer's logic correct?
4. What other evidence is offered?
5. Are you convinced by this editorial? Whether yes or no, give the principal reason.

An assignment of this kind must be followed by ample time for follow-up discussion.

The amount of time required by critique groups varies widely according to the length of the assignment, the size of the groups, and the general level of competence in the class. Paragraph analysis may take as little as fifteen or twenty minutes, but an exercise based on a three-hundred-word composition will almost always take close to forty minutes. Time must also be allowed for follow-up clarification and discussion. An assignment including questions which are subject to varied interpretation (such as the editorial exercise above) needs more follow-up time than does one that is concerned primarily with mechanics (such as subject-verb agreement). Time requirements may also be reduced as students develop critical skills. They will need more time for something new, less for something they've had some practice in, but it's better to allow more time than turns out to be necessary than to run out of time before groups have satisfactorily completed an exercise.

When all desired revisions are made, or when final drafts have been completed, papers are turned in, with or without their feedback sheets. The teacher can then read, grade, and comment on the papers and the critical analyses according to whatever principles he or she wishes. The important work, however, has already been done. Each student has written a composition and revised it (if necessary) in the light of critical comments from an audience of peers, and each student has read and thought about several other papers from a particular critical viewpoint. Furthermore, each author-critic has had the opportunity to engage in the give and take of follow-up discussion with other author-critics and to receive expert advice from the teacher if desired. Of course, written commentary and evaluation from the teacher will provide additional feedback to the writer, but quite enough has been accomplished if the teacher merely records what has been done and places the papers in the students' folders.

Peer Proofreading

Irene Payan
Neguanee High School, Michigan

One of my most successful teaching tactics concerns proofreading, but it can be used for any kind of lesson that lends itself to peer discussion. The game is called "Clock," and it is as successful and enjoyable when used with high school seniors as it is among freshmen.

Realizing that peer approval is most important and that one learns much by teaching, I have my students proofread each other's work (themes, poems, or whatever, but not tests) before submitting their final drafts. Students' desks are arranged in two concentric circles, ovals, or squares, depending on the size of the group and the shape of the classroom. Half the class occupies the seats arranged in the inner circle, facing out, thus making the "face" of the clock. Each of the remaining students stands in front of a seated person; we call these students "hands." Whenever there is an uneven number of students, I become part of the "face." The desks of the outer circle are used for writing or leaning.

Before we begin I repeat the objective of the assignment and the list of details we will be checking. As I call out the first detail to be checked, the seated student and his or her partner read each other's paper. Every time we consider a different detail, the standing student moves to the left to advance the clock "one hour," or one student. Students now consider the next item on the list with a new partner. After a few minutes, when most people seem to have finished glancing through their partner's paper, we advance another hour. We do not wait till everyone has finished reading every word because we cannot allow the procedure to degenerate into an hour of socializing.

If the assignment concerned the use of descriptive techniques, like appeal to the senses, physical point of view, or figures of speech, I have each technique reviewed separately. When time

124

permits we proofread for stylistic details, such as effective beginnings or endings. We always allow time at the end of the hour to check on mechanics.

I am positive that a student's advice is often more well-received than mine. Furthermore, students will point out errors that I may want to overlook tactfully—to spare frustration. Sometimes students help each other with situations that were not called out. The technique also makes a few realize that the first draft of a paper is rarely a perfect composition. Be it teacher or student, one learns much from an exchange of ideas, in regard to content as well as form.

Peer Evaluation: One Approach

Mary Louise Foster
Tulane University

Patricia Markey Naranjo
Tulane University

University instructors burdened with large classes are often unable to evaluate several drafts of a paper; consequently, students often remain unaware of the need for close rereadings and revisions of their work. Believing that many composition instructors seek less exhausting alternatives to evaluation than copious written comments and lengthy individual conferences, we would like to suggest a technique that has worked well in our classes. This simple method of peer evaluation teaches students the processes of close reading and revision, uses little extra instructor time, and produces a small but effective student audience which generates constructive, independent evaluations of each class member's work. These evaluations do not replace an instructor's grades and comments on the final drafts of papers. They do provide, however, valuable intermediary appraisals of preliminary drafts and therefore encourage clearer, more effective writing.

We set aside a class session as an evaluation period and begin by emphasizing the advantages of learning how others react to one's writing. We then establish guidelines for the evaluation. Sometimes we ask students to summarize a fellow student's essay in one to three sentences and then to write one or two further observations about it. At other times we distribute a three-point guide: (1) What is the writer trying to say? (2) Is the form correct and the paper grammatical? (3) Is the paper interesting, and what could the writer do to improve it? We request that every student set a goal—perhaps to read and criticize five student essays before the class period ends. We ask that all comments be made on a blank sheet, with the remarks intended for each classmate designated by name or by prearranged code (the author's date of birth, for example). When a student finishes a paper, he or she gives it to someone in the class who is ready to begin another one. In a typical medium-to-large class rarely does a student have to wait for a paper.

The sessions are a little noisy as classmates request and exchange essays; nevertheless, they are very rewarding. At the end of the period every student has completed a comment sheet with five or six separate small paragraphs, each designated for a different classmate. We pick up these sheets and the essays. Later we cut the comment sheets apart and paste or tape all the remarks intended for one person onto a single sheet of paper. At the next class meeting each student receives his or her essay and the observations of five or six classmates.

This form of peer evaluation has several advantages over the more common approach of making multiple copies of students' papers. In the first place, it uses instructor time more efficiently: the time expended typing a student essay onto a stencil and reproducing it results in a critique of only one paper, while our technique produces critiques of all the papers in the class.

In addition, our method produces peer critiques that are more objective. Because critiques are not made in front of the class, there is far less "herd effect": students do not merely second a persuasive student's opinion, nor do they tend to be impressed by pretentious and empty papers simply because they were read by readers with a flair for drama. Also, the students cannot take cues from the instructor's comments, facial expression, or tone of voice before they decide what they think about a paper. In fact, our realization of a need for increased peer objectivity was the basis for our decisions not to make comments on the papers before the class evaluation session, not to allow students to write on the papers themselves, and not to have a single evaluation sheet passed around with each theme. As a result of these decisions, no student can tell what elements in a paper others have criticized or applauded.

Cut-and-paste comment sheets also improve student morale. Since we urge students to read an entire paper before they begin to comment, the criticisms are generally balanced and useful and only rarely sarcastic or cruel. Written comments greatly reduce that sense of threat that students face during class critiques, and the shy student, who feels self-conscious speaking before the class, is free to react to the work of others without forfeiting privacy.

Our method avoids a censorious group atmosphere. The class never seems bored, uncomfortable, or hostile during the written evaluation session—in part, we believe, because the format gives all students a chance to participate while preserving their anonymity.

Not only does this form of peer evaluation encourage objectivity and authentic response, but it is also useful in teaching and reinforcing specific writing skills. For example, students can be asked to evaluate types of arguments, to watch for concrete details, to note vivid descriptions, to consider audience needs. Guidelines may also be used to introduce a new writing skill. As the session begins, the instructor distributes specific evaluation questions that emphasize a new skill, the importance of the introduction or conclusion, for example. Students then evaluate how their classmates have approached this aspect of writing in their current papers.

While the traditional group method of evaluating a single essay can accomplish any of these teaching goals, it can accomplish them only for students who are willing to participate fully in the class discussion by listening carefully, offering comments, and evaluating the comments of others. In actual practice not every student in the class can or will participate in an open discussion, and many of those who do join in spend portions of the session daydreaming. By providing each student with a definite goal—five written evaluations—our method discourages wasting time. Students actually spend more time concentrating on the task at hand; consequently, their error recognition skills improve as does their ability to read papers for clarity and organization.

The technique works well for a draft of a short paper or for a crucial portion, the introduction or conclusion, perhaps, of a longer paper. It can also be used for in-class paragraph exercises or to elicit lively student evaluations of instructor-written "freshman" essays. The procedure works as well for papers about literary subjects as it does for those on current issues or personal reflections. In the case of literature classes, whether or not each member of the class has read the literary work discussed in a given paper is largely immaterial since clarity of communication is the point of address. If a student cannot summarize what another student has written, he or she has probably detected a problem of logic or development.

Regardless of subject matter, in-class peer evaluation is most helpful to both students and instructors at the rough or first draft stage. The prospect of a future grade and the opportunity to improve that grade insures that each student will weigh the returned comments carefully. It is also at this crucial point that the procedure can relieve the teacher of one tedious reading step and thus hours of work. Consequently, a teacher can require two or three drafts of an important paper where large class loads and other responsibilities would normally force him or her to call for only one draft. Indeed, this approach to peer evaluation can make each new writing assignment truly the beginning of a process, not simply a demand for a finished product in two weeks. Indeed, many students review work carefully and plan multiple rewrites for the first time. In a real sense such planning marks the beginning of their growth as writers, for one difference between beginners and experienced writers is that the latter are more flexible, more willing to arrange and rearrange words, sentences, even paragraphs or whole essay sections in the interests of clarity and style. Student responsibility for initial criticisms of peer essays not only saves the teacher's time but also—and most importantly—makes students perform the tasks that all good writers do: careful reading and evaluation of copy and thoughtful planning for revisions.

Finally, we would like to mention how quickly this exercise gives students a feel for good, bad, and average compositions. Because students read five or six papers in rapid succession and because they ask the same questions about each essay, they get a sense of the relative value of one paper compared to another. With this increased awareness, students are often better able to deal with their own grades. As teachers have always realized, students who read only their own work are unlikely to believe it can be improved. As teachers also know, students who feel their writing in under attack from the class are likely to be defensive, too concerned with protecting themselves and justifying their papers to think constructively about improving them. Cut-and-paste comment sheets permit students to keep their dignity while receiving important criticisms from their classmates.

Structuring Peer Evaluation for Greater Student Independence

Neil Ellman
Hanover Park Regional High School District, New Jersey

One of the most effective ways of teaching composition while at the same time reducing a teacher's paper load is peer evaluation. While terminal grading remains the prerogative of the teacher under such a system, the students themselves assume the function of providing immediately useful feedback to their peers. The benefit is not only to the teacher but also to the students, who write for an audience of peers, receive feedback from a source less threatening than teachers, and have the opportunity to develop independent critical skills.

Although peer evaluation systems can and do work in a wide range of classroom settings, many teachers still do not believe that students are skilled enough to offer meaningful feedback nor mature enough to be fair, objective, concrete, and constructive in their criticism. To some extent, this cynicism is warranted, not because students cannot be effective peer evaluators, but because they have neither experience nor training in peer evaluation procedures.

In order for peer evaluation to work properly, and thus relieve the teacher of the burden of providing all feedback, students must be trained to be effective, independent peer evaluators. The training process must be structured, sequential, and deliberate, for the teacher cannot expect students to acquire the necessary skills and assume an adequate level of responsibility in a short time.

For purposes of example, let us assume that a class of twenty-five students has been divided into five groups. Each student initiates a composition, and it is the responsibility of each other member of the group to read the composition and to provide the author with feedback useful enough to be utilized in revising the composition. To be able to provide such feedback, a four-phase training sequence is recommended.

130

Checklist Response. The initial phase of peer evaluation should be structured in such a way that students need only recognize the presence or absence of specified qualities of written composition. A checklist based on concepts taught in class should be presented to each student.

> After reading the introductory paragraph, do you have a good idea of what the author intends to say in the composition?
>
> Does the beginning of the composition make you want to continue reading?
>
> Does each paragraph have a topic sentence?
>
> Does the author use only simple sentences?

This procedure introduces students to the qualities of effective composition, enables them to make simple yes/no judgments, and provides feedback for the author. As the teacher introduces new qualities, the checklist is expanded. Thus, at the beginning of this phase, the checklist may be short and simple, containing such questions as "Does the author vary the length of sentences?" Later, the checklist may be longer and contain more complex questions such as, "Is there a logical sequence of ideas?"

Checklist Response with Comments. When students have learned to recognize the qualities of effective composition, they should be encouraged to express their personal reactions and to offer constructive criticism. Structurally, this step requires that each yes or no response on the checklist be supported by a specific reference to the text and by an explanation (in the case of a "yes") or by a constructive alternative (in the case of a "no"). Intellectually, this step also requires that students be able to form and apply such concepts as specificity and concreteness. A teacher cannot expect a student to be concrete in making critical comments unless the student has formed this concept and is thus able to recognize concreteness.

In order to develop such concepts in students, the teacher should stage a model peer evaluation sequence. A first run-through can be provided solely by the teacher, and a second can involve the students themselves in a simulated exercise. In each case, specific and nonspecific, concrete and nonconcrete, and constructive and nonconstructive comments are presented, analyzed, and categorized. Only when these concepts have been attained can students be expected to apply them to new and unfamiliar pieces of writing. The monitoring of such application, rather than the provision of the feedback itself, then becomes the chief function of the teacher in the peer evaluation process.

Open-Ended Response. There comes a time, of course, when students no longer require the formal structure of a checklist. When they have internalized the qualities of effective written composition and formed the concepts necessary for effective feedback, students should be ready to provide open-ended criticism. For some teachers, this is the objective toward which the training process is directed. Allow me to suggest a higher objective.

Peer Revision. It is one thing for students to be able to offer constructive alternatives; it is another to be able to act upon such alternatives. Consider this procedure: after the original author writes a short composition, each other member of the group, instead of merely offering criticism, rewrites the composition incorporating his or her own suggestions. The amount of writing is increased for all students without the necessity for additional grading. Cooperative behavior is encouraged, and the original author has the benefit of highly specific alternatives from which to choose. Although the procedure is similar to group composition, the outcome is different, for the original author, whose judgment and choices determine the shape of the final paper, retains the responsibility of authorship.

Exploiting Reality in the Journalism Classroom

Lawrence B. Fuller
Bloomsburg State College

Anyone who has taught introductory journalism effectively has had to devise ways to handle the paper load generated by such courses. In the past eight years I have developed the following approach as a way to give fast feedback for the more than 500 articles that two sections of introductory level college students write in a semester.

First, I require that all articles be typed according to the format found in our journalism textbook. Some students initially complain that they can't type or don't have typewriters, but I am inflexible because newspapers require mastery of the keyboard whether one works as a reporter or submits publicity. Equally important, typed copy is much easier for me and other students to read than handwriting.

Second, I describe the type and content of all articles and publish their deadlines early in the semester so that students will have ample time to gather information and consult with me about problems they encounter. Missing a deadline penalizes a grade except when unavoidable emergencies like sickness, a death in the family, or a source's schedule interfere. I ask students to inform me about such emergencies before the deadline, if possible. This policy reduces the chances of a student's falling behind and turning articles in late in the semester when my reading load is likely to be heavy.

Third, on days when articles are due, I divide the class into groups of three or four, often on a random basis to break up cliques, and have the students spend twenty minutes editing each other's articles. Any changes made at this point do not count against the grade I eventually assign the article. Any corrections one student suggests to another can have a positive effect. Usually the groups catch most errors in spelling, punctuation, agreement, and parallel structure.

This editing work has several benefits. It introduces the class members to each other and shows them how writing can be a collective effort. It enables each student to get immediate feedback from two or three students. It allows each student to compare his or her work with that submitted by peers. It permits last-minute, handwritten revision.

Fourth, I encourage students to submit articles they prepare for class to the college newspaper as well. My carrot is my promise to give any article published in any paper a grade of at least "B," even though my initial evaluation may have been lower. Of even greater importance is my desire to involve student editors of the paper in the process of evaluating the work of my students. Often they will make comments about an article that I would hesitate to make for fear of intimidating the student.

Fifth, after the groups have edited each other's work in class, I randomly select several articles for class examination on the opaque projector. In this part of the evaluation I am concerned as much about what the editors have done as about what the writers have written. Writers explain why they wrote as they did; editors defend their changes. Other members of the class and I point out problems that both have ignored. To avoid bruising egos too much, I make sure that each class member goes through this public examination once before I use a student's work a second time. Besides giving students a further reaction to their work, these public examinations accustom them to discussing their writing openly.

Sixth, after all of this discussion, I finally read the articles, note any problems not previously mentioned, and write a detailed comment analyzing how the student succeeded or failed. I try to return all articles within a week, and usually succeed. Generally there is a noticeable improvement in grades as the semester passes that reflects the students' increasing mastery of the various practices peculiar to journalism.

This particular pattern has evolved primarily because the climax of the introductory journalism course, the final examination, requires each section to publish one issue of the campus newspaper. To do this successfully students must master the various conventions, practices, and attitudes of journalists so that I can limit my advisory role to editorial problems of layout, libel, newsworthiness, and accuracy. Otherwise, deadline nights would be disasters lasting into the early morning with me doing most of the work. By insisting on typing and meeting deadlines, by encouraging long-term preparation of articles, by viewing articles as public documents once submitted, and by encouraging ongoing criticism of reporters' and editors' decisions from the beginning, I usually find that each section's issue of the paper is as good as or better than the issues produced by the regular staff.

Most semesters I find that by midterm I am looking forward to reading most of my students' articles because I am being informed in a generally clear manner about all sorts of interesting matters. Well-written articles make my reading load quite manageable and allow me to concentrate on those students who have serious difficulties.